# Lynne Edwards'
## ◆◆ *NEW* ◆◆
# SAMPLER QUILT
## BOOK

# Lynne Edwards'
## ❖ *NEW* ❖
# SAMPLER QUILT
## BOOK

David & Charles

*To Brian.*
*To my parents.*
*To Dickon and to Tom, Angela and Holly.*
*Also to the memory of Ann Pepprell, some of whose fabric appears in my quilt.*
*To all the quilters who have used the first Sampler Quilt Book and found it helpful. They have waited patiently for this second book – I hope they feel it is worth the waiting! Finally to the quilters who have made the Hall in Chelsworth the centre of my activities over the past eight years. Not many people can do what they enjoy and get paid for it. I am to be envied.*

(page 2) Lynne Edwards' New Sampler Quilt

A DAVID & CHARLES BOOK

First published in the UK in 2000

Text and designs Copyright © Lynne Edwards 2000
Photography and layout © David & Charles 2000

A catalogue record for this book is available from the British Library.

ISBN 0 7153 0956 0

Photography by The Photographic Workshop
and Jon Stewart
Book design by Maggie Aldred
Printed in Italy by Lego Spa
for David & Charles
Brunel House    Newton Abbot    Devon

# CONTENTS

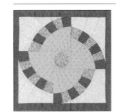

# INTRODUCTION

For some years I have run a one-year course on making a sampler quilt, with students gradually learning all the various hand and machine techniques necessary to complete a sampler quilt. This book, like the first *Sampler Quilt Book,* was devised from that course.

When the first *Sampler Quilt Book* was published students became very nostalgic about the course they had toiled through in past years. Misty-eyed they declared that they had never learned so much nor achieved so much as then. They had, of course, forgotten how hard they had worked. . . Couldn't they do another course, a more advanced one, with all the blocks and techniques that had not been covered in the first quilt?

So that was the start of this *New Sampler Quilt Book,* based on the course which more than a hundred willing victims undertook. The course proved to be even more work than the first one, but because the blocks were more complex (although not necessarily more difficult), the resulting quilts are richer and even more impressive – real heirlooms to be treasured.

A sampler quilt is an ideal way to try twenty different techniques without ending up with a pile of unfinished samples. Skills are acquired for future projects and new techniques become unexpected favourites. Others may fall into the 'never again'

category, but at least you have found out that it's not for you. The blocks are framed and then quilted individually before being joined together in the 'quilt-as-you-go' technique. I used this method for the first *Sampler Quilt Book* and although the final joining together can be tedious, it does mean that the quilting is easier and more portable and the quilts do get finished.

The blocks are a mixture of hand and machine work and are sequenced in order so that the skills learned from one block may be used in other later block designs. This is the same order that I teach for the course of the New Sampler Quilt and you can simply follow it from beginning to end as the students do. Alternatively you can dip into the book, choosing designs or techniques that appeal to you and make single blocks which can be used with others or on their own in your personal projects.

Many of the quilts shown include extra blocks chosen and constructed by the students without my help, either because they omitted some of mine or because they needed more blocks for their king-sized quilts. If these are the very blocks that you really want to make, then I apologise. The trouble with giving students more skills and the confidence to pursue their own ideas is that they do just that, whether I like it or not. . .

# GETTING STARTED

Basic equipment is described on page 8 but questions about fabric and batting need to be discussed first.

### HOW MUCH FABRIC DO I NEED?

For a single bed quilt you will need a total of about 6yd (5.5m) of 45in (115cm) wide fabric for the front of the quilt. For a double bed quilt about 9yd (8.25m) is needed. To begin with it is better to buy small amounts, 1/2yd (45.7cm) or so, of six to eight fabrics and then see how the quilt develops. This is risky I know, but if you have bought three yards of one fabric you will feel obliged to use it, even if the quilt is moving in another direction where that particular fabric does not belong. Once a few blocks have been made you will be able to add fabrics more easily, as you will see which fabrics and colours are working well together. If one of your favourites is no longer available, find another similar in colour, which will add to the richness of the quilt. You will be surprised how far 1/2yd (45.7cm) will go.

With the 'quilt-as-you-go' technique, a whole piece of fabric for the backing is not required as each block is backed individually. For this New Sampler Quilt, each of the blocks is backed with a square of fabric 17 1/2 x 17 1/2in (44.5 x 44.5cm), so you can cut these as you go along. As a guide you need 6yd (5.5m) of 45in (115cm) wide backing fabric for a single bed quilt and about 8yd (7.3cm) for all twenty blocks plus borders. This is a lot of fabric, so shop around for something you like that is not too expensive. I used one backing fabric for the blocks and another to back the borders which means I get patchwork on both sides of the quilt.

### HOW DO I CHOOSE COLOURS?

Colour is very personal and is strongly influenced by fashion but it is probably best to start with a fabric you really like. If you want your quilt to be essentially one colour then make sure there is plenty of variation in the shades you use, both light and dark. If you want a real contrast of colours, like a red and white quilt, add textures, spots, checks and small and large prints to the basic red and white scheme.

The New Sampler Quilt is quite complex in design and probably looks best with a limited number of colours. Begin by choosing one fabric in a colour you really want to use and then find two or three more that are similar. Try to stick to medium-weight cotton fabrics for the quilt, as these are easier to handle and to use together. A mix of patterned and plain or slightly textured fabrics will give balance to the quilt.

Many of the blocks have a background area that supports the main design. Find a fabric that will look good in a supporting role with your first collection. I used two similar creamy-beige fabrics for my background areas (see picture on page 2), but one would do to begin with and you may decide in time to keep to that one fabric throughout. Finally, take all your chosen pieces and pick a third colour and even a fourth if you wish that will add some interest to the quilt. Small amounts of several fabrics will allow you to build up a palette of shades to dip into as you choose for each block. Bear in mind that the main area of regret with students is that they have not restricted their palette of colours enough but have added more and more as they went along.

### WHAT ABOUT THE BATTING?

The amount of batting needed – the layer of padding between the front and back of the quilt – will be similar to the fabric backing. There are now more options for batting available. This time round I used an heirloom batting 80% cotton 20% polyester, which was a joy to quilt. It is much thinner than the usual two ounce polyester but made a much heavier quilt. Take the advice of other quilters when choosing a batting. A factor to be considered is how much you intend to quilt your blocks, as some battings specify quite close areas of quilting while others allow large spaces between quilt lines.

### HOW DO I PREPARE THE FABRICS?

It is safest to wash all fabrics before use. However, if, like me, you enjoy working with fresh, crisp unwashed fabrics, you must at least test any strong or dark fabrics for colourfastness before you begin. Wash these separately with a gentle non-biological liquid soap or detergent and check that the colour does not leak out into the water. Reds, indigo and dark browns are all colours to be tested as they can be the ruin of your quilt. Specialist quilt fabrics are not likely to shrink, but I am not so sure about furnishing cottons or fashion fabrics and always wash them before use. Try to iron the fabrics while they are still slightly damp to ensure a smooth finish.

# BASIC EQUIPMENT

There is an increasingly wide range of tools and gadgets available from specialist shops and quilt shows. If you are a beginner it is probably best to stick to the basic equipment listed here.

## FOR HAND-SEWING

**Needles:** Try to buy packets of one size only – it's more economical. Sharps size 9 or 10 are best for piecing and appliqué. Betweens size 9 or 10 are best for quilting.

**Pins:** My current favourite are silk pins which are very fine but strong. Otherwise I use long, fine dressmaker's pins (extra-fine, extra-long), although other people favour the coloured, glass-headed type as they are easier to hold and find. Buy the smaller, fine variety rather than huge quilt pins.

**Thimble:** The use of a thimble is your choice but I feel that one is needed for quilting, to protect the middle finger of your dominant hand. A flat-topped one is the best shape.

**Thread:** For sewing cotton fabrics I like to use a good quality, pure cotton thread, although cotton-coated polyester is a good alternative. Try to match the colour of the thread as closely as possible to the fabrics. If using a mixture of colours, it is best to go for a darker rather than a lighter shade. For quilting, pure cotton quilting thread is ideal. It is stronger, thicker and waxed to give a smooth thread that tangles less than ordinary sewing thread.

**Scissors:** You will need a sharp, medium-sized pair of scissors for cutting fabric, plus a larger pair for paper cutting. A pair of small, sharp scissors with good points will be useful for clipping seams and trimming thread.

**Fabric Markers:** You will need a fabric marker to mark template shapes on to fabric and indicate quilting lines. Beware of spirit pens though, even if water erasable. They make a harsh line and it is not known yet whether their chemicals will eventually rot fabric. Specialist quilt shops sell silver, white and yellow marking pencils which can be sharpened to a fine point. Read the packaging carefully before you use them; if it says 'will not fade' it's fine for marking around templates but is not suitable for quilting. Always test the marker on a spare piece of fabric before you start work and check it can be erased. You can buy a fabric eraser for use with these markers. For quilting I use Aquarelle coloured pencils in the softest quality, bought from art shops. Choose a shade similar to the fabric but dark enough to be seen clearly. The line wears off the fabric as it is worked and can be sponged if necessary to remove final traces.

**Tape Measure:** Use an extra long tape measure – 100in (2.5m) or longer with metric markings on the reverse.

**Bias Bars:** These are produced specifically for Celtic patchwork, where narrow strips of fabric are appliquéd on a background in interlaced patterns. There are several widths of bar, from $1/8$in (3mm) to $1/2$in (1.2cm). A $1/4$in (6mm) bar is used for the Celtic Knot block, and a narrower $1/8$in (3mm) bar for the Celtic Appliqué block.

**Masking Tape:** Special $1/4$in (6mm) masking tape is sold in quilt shops which is really useful for marking straight lines for quilting. Avoid the wider varieties sold in stationers and do-it-yourself shops as they are not low-tack. Do not leave any tape on the fabric any longer than necessary just in case it leaves a mark.

## FOR MAKING THE TEMPLATES

Many of the block designs use templates transferred on to card or template plastic. Accuracy is critical so you will need very sharp pencils, pencil sharpener, eraser, ruler, tracing paper and card or template plastic.

Template plastic is widely available from specialist quilt shops and other sewing equipment outlets. It can be used over and over again. The plastic is clear and firm, yet pliable and easy to cut with scissors. It is available in two types: a plain, clear one, and one marked with a measured grid.

Graph paper is very useful for drafting your own patterns and borders. Quilt shops often have A4 pads marked in $1/4$in (6mm) squares. Art shops usually stock large sheets of graph paper marked in inches, but beware of buying any with $1/10$in (2.5mm) markings, as they don't show the $1/4$in (6mm) divisions.

**Freezer Paper:** This is becoming very popular in the USA for appliqué work. It looks like grease-proof paper but is slightly thicker and has a shiny side which sticks to the fabric when it is ironed. Thus it keeps small appliqué shapes firm as they are stitched in place. After use the paper can be peeled off without leaving any marks and reused. Currently freezer paper is only available from specialist quilt shops. A good substitute is the thick paper used to wrap packs of photocopying paper.

## FOR MACHINE WORK

**Sewing Machine:** This does not have to be a state of the art model, just a reliable one you enjoy using. Use a size 11/80 needle for medium-weight cotton fabrics and change after at least every eight sewing hours. A straight-stitch foot is ideal for machine patchwork. You need to stitch straight seams that are exactly 1/4in (6mm) from the needle, so a narrow straight-stitch foot is very helpful. So too is the 1/4in (6mm) foot that some manufacturers have produced especially for quilters. A walking foot is useful for stitching through layers of fabric and batting, as it prevents the top fabric from creeping ahead of the other layers and giving a twisted effect. It also makes sewing on the final binding to the quilt much easier and is essential for machine quilting.

**Thread:** Use the same cotton or cotton-coated polyester thread as for hand-sewing. Choose one manufacturer and type of thread and stick to this throughout for both top and bobbin thread.

**Stitch Ripper:** I use this as an extra finger to hold fabric in place while feeding it under the machine foot. It can also prevent the seam allowances from being pushed in the wrong direction by the machine foot as you sew.

**Pins:** For any machine work I prefer silk pins or extra-fine, extra-long pins as they slip out of the fabric so easily.

## FOR ROTARY CUTTING

Once you start using a rotary cutter, ruler and mat, you will wonder how you ever managed without them. There are several different mats on the market, but do get one with an inch grid marked on. The most useful size for patchwork is the larger one, 23 x 17in (58.5 x 43cm). Always follow the instructions printed on the mat: store flat out of direct sunlight. The mat is self-healing when a rotary cutter is used on it. Do use the appropriate cutter as craft knives as other blades do real damage.

Cutters come in two sizes, with the small one cutting up to four layers of fabric. I own both large and small cutters which I use for different tasks. The blades do get blunt with use and must be replaced at intervals.

Special rulers must be used with the mat and cutter because the cutter will shave off the edges of wooden, metal and plastic rulers. Rotary rulers are about 1/8in (3mm) thick and are made of tough acrylic. Choose one with markings that you feel comfortable reading and which measures up to 24in (61cm). This size will work well on folded fabric and on a medium-sized cutting mat. A 12 1/2in (31.7cm) square Perspex ruler is also useful.

## OTHER USEFUL ITEMS

**Display Board:** A piece of white felt or flannelette stretched over a board is good for planning your designs, as the cut pieces will 'stick' to the fabric without pins. A large cork or polystyrene tile also works well, but with these you will need pins to keep the pieces in position.

**Light Box:** A light box for tracing designs on to fabric can be bought from business supply shops, but is very expensive. All you really need is a flat, clear surface lit from below so that lines to be traced are highlighted through the fabric. A glass-topped table with a light beneath will give the same effect. If all else fails, tape the design to a window, tape the fabric over the top and trace the outline.

# BASIC TECHNIQUES

This section looks at some of the basic techniques you need to master to make the New Sampler Quilt.

## MAKING TEMPLATES

The blocks in this sampler quilt use specific shapes joined together to create the design. These shapes are provided with the individual block instructions and should be made into templates to be used as required. Templates are made by tracing a shape and transferring it on to card or special template plastic. If using card, first trace the shape on to tracing paper. When tracing a straight-lined shape such as a diamond, mark the corners with a dot and carefully join the dots with a ruler and a sharp pencil. Mark the arrow to show the direction of the grain of the fabric. Cut out the traced shape roughly, keeping about 1/4in (6mm) outside the drawn outline. Stick this on to card and then cut out the exact outline through both tracing paper and card. Cut just inside the drawn lines as this keeps the measurements accurate as you draw round the template on the fabric.

If using template plastic, trace over the outline and grain arrow in the way described above. Cut out the template carefully with scissors, again cutting just inside the lines to keep the measurements accurate. Label each template clearly and put them all in an envelope or transparent wallet so that you can use them again.

## PRESSING

A good iron and ironing board are essential for all sewing work. Press all your fabric before use, as creased fabric leads to inaccuracy. When pressing seams in patchwork, press from the front and use a dry iron as steam can distort, especially on bias seams. Resist the temptation to press seams in patchwork from the back – you could press little pleats in the fabric over the seams which you only discover when you turn the piece over to the front. These tiny, roll-over creases are hard to press out and can lead to inaccuracy.

## SETTING UP THE MACHINE

It is important to have your sewing machine and chair at the right height and an adjustable office chair might be a good investment. If you cannot leave your sewing machine permanently in position, do all the preliminary cutting work first and then clear a space for the machine.

Thread the machine ready for use. If it has an extension plate that fits on to create a larger surface, do use it as it supports the patchwork and stops it from pulling away from the needle as you stitch. Set the stitch length to a shorter stitch than required for dressmaking – about two-thirds the usual size or about fifteen stitches to the inch. This will be small enough to prevent the seams from coming undone when they are cut, but not so small that you can't unpick them.

Many people find stitching a straight line very difficult. If you fit a 1/4in (6mm) foot on your machine, it really will help. One trick is to stick a strip of masking tape on to the machine exactly 1/4in (6mm) away from the needle. This makes a good edge to line your fabric against as you sew. Use the point of a stitch ripper to help guide the fabric accurately while stitching.

There is a useful test to find out whether your 1/4in (6mm) seam is accurate. The seam may be just right mathematically but because the seams are pressed to one side rather than pressed open, it makes the seams a tiny bit wider, so you need to stitch a slightly 'skinny' 1/4in (6mm) to finish up with the correct sizing.

Take a strip of one of your fabrics 2in (5cm) wide and about 18in (45.7cm) long and cut it into three lengths (Fig 1a). Stitch these three lengths together with a 1/4in (6mm) seam. Press the seams to one side, from the front of the work so that the seams are really flat (Fig 1b). Now measure the work from side to side, it should be exactly 5in (12.7cm). If it is smaller than this your seams are too wide; if it is

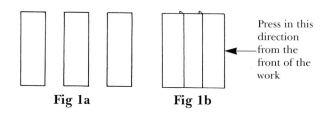

**Fig 1a**          **Fig 1b**

Press in this direction from the front of the work

more than 5in (12.7cm) your seams are too narrow. Try the test again, adjusting the position of your masking tape until you get exactly the right seam allowance. Once this has been done you are set up for all your future patchwork.

## ROTARY CUTTING

To cut fabric, place it on the cutting mat and align the woven threads of the fabric (called the grain) with the gridlines on the mat. Position the ruler on the fabric and hold it firmly so your hand forms an arch and is not lying flat, as there is more strength in your fingers than in the flat of your hand. Hold the handle at an angle of 45° to the mat, not leaning to one side or the other. The flatter side of the cutter should be against the side of the ruler, not the side with the assembly nut (see photograph below). Only snap down the safety guard when you are ready to cut. Left-handed users should cut from the left side rather than from the right. Get into the habit of always cutting *away* from you, so start at the near side of the mat and begin cutting before the blade reaches the fabric, pressing down

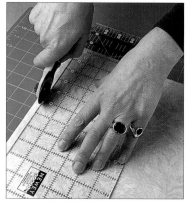

firmly and evenly in one continuous movement. If the ruler has a tendency to slip to one side as you cut, stop cutting and move your hand crab-like up the ruler before starting to cut again.

### Cutting Strips

Remember that strips cut from the width of the fabric will be stretchy, so whenever possible cut strips down the side parallel to the selvedge. If you are working with more than a couple of yards or metres of fabric, cutting from the long side of the fabric will also keep the length intact for use in borders later.

**1** Turn the cutting mat so that the longer side runs from top to bottom to give a longer cutting distance. If the piece of fabric is too long for the mat, fold it carefully as many times as needed to make it fit on to the cutting mat with the selvedge edges exactly on top of each other. Place the fabric on the mat with the folded edge along a *horizontal* gridline. This is very important to avoid getting V-shapes in the final long strip.

**2** Place the ruler on one of the *vertical* gridlines on the mat and trim off the selvedges. To cut a strip of a measured width use the marked measurements at the top and bottom of the mat. I actually count the number of inches along the top markings on the mat. Move the ruler to this position, hold it firmly and cut along its edge. Before moving the ruler, check that all the layers have been completely cut through. If not, re-cut the whole strip rather than saw at the offending section.

**3** Lift the ruler and reposition it for cutting the next strip. Continue to cut until the necessary number of strips have been cut.

### An Alternative Method for Cutting Strips

When cutting strips or drawing a grid for quick pieced triangles, measurements like $3^7/8$in (9.8cm) are quite common. It is all too easy to mis-measure when using the mat markings as a guide. Instead, after trimming the selvedges, turn the mat through 180° without disturbing the fabric, or walk around the mat to the other side. Start cutting from the left-hand side instead of from the right. If you are left-handed just reverse these directions. Pass the ruler over the cut edge until the fabric edge lines up with the required measurement on the ruler itself (see photograph below). Cut along the ruler's right side and remove the cut strip. Move the ruler across the fabric until the new cut edge matches up with the required measurement on the ruler and cut once more. Continue to do this across the fabric as many times as required.

### Cutting a Square

If the fabric will fit on to the mat without hanging over the edge, place it down with the grain parallel to the mat's gridlines. Straighten one edge of the fabric by lining the ruler up with a vertical gridline and cutting against it. Without moving the fabric, cut a second vertical line at the desired distance from the first one (count the squares to check). Turn the mat through 90° and trim the other two sides of the square the same way.

If the piece of fabric is too big for the mat, you could cut out the square roughly first and then trim it on the mat as described above or alternatively use one of the large square rulers. Place a corner of the fabric on the mat, matching the fabric grain with the mat's gridlines. Position the square ruler on it with about 1/2in (1.2cm) of fabric to spare on two sides. Trim along these sides with the cutter (see photograph below). Turn the square so that the diagonal line marked 0 is at the trimmed corner.

Move it across the cut edges until the chosen measurement on the two sides of the ruler lines up with the cut edges (see photograph below). Trim the remaining two sides to complete the square. In this way the square is cut with little waste.

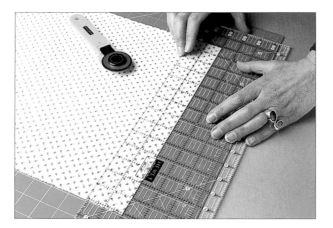

# MAKING THE BLOCKS

Each block for the New Sampler Quilt is fully described, with guidance in selecting colours and fabrics, step-by-step instructions, and clear diagrams throughout. Look at the photographs of students' quilts throughout the book to get some ideas for your own colour schemes. The blocks are presented in sequence so the skills learned in one design are built upon in following blocks, and probably the best way to use the book is to work through the blocks one by one. However, feel free to leave out blocks that do not appeal or to make more of the ones you really love. It is, after all, *your* quilt and you are allowed to pick and choose. The advantage of making and quilting the blocks individually and then assembling them at the end is that you can decide how many to make. Whether they finish up as a huge king-size quilt, a cot quilt or just a series of cushions is up to you.

# INNER CITY

Everyone knows the traditional hexagon shape – it's how most people start patchwork and often, alas, where they also stop. The process of cutting fabric and papers and then laboriously stitching the fabric over the papers before joining these to make a design is slow and does not offer much short-term gratification, especially if the colours and arrangements of hexagons have no planned design. This has meant that the recent upsurge of interest in patchwork has tended to bypass the

hexagon in favour of quicker and more exciting techniques. Still, the hexagon shape can be used to create wonderful heirloom quilts following the English Patchwork tradition. The flower-like arrangement of six hexagons placed around a central hexagon, called Grandmother's Flower Garden (Fig 1), is the most popular design and when the colours are controlled and arranged in an overall design on the quilt, the result is pure pleasure.

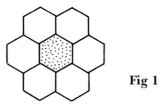

**Fig 1**

The hexagon can also be used in exciting contemporary designs like this Inner City block chosen for the first block in the New Sampler Quilt. This design is based on a hexagon made in the traditional English Patchwork method over paper, but the construction and arrangement are slightly different and result in the elegant three-dimensional design known as Inner City.

### COLOUR CHOICES

Like Tumbling Blocks, this design has a three-dimensional effect that is achieved by using three fabrics – one light (L), one medium (M) and one dark (D). Arrange the three fabrics next to each other on a surface to check whether there is enough definition between them. It needs to be fairly obvious which fabric is lighter than the others and which is the dark choice. The medium fabric will lie somewhere between these two extremes. Looking through half-closed eyes at the fabrics helps to see the difference in tones. A fourth fabric is needed for the background to the design. Sometimes it helps to leave the decision about the background until the Inner City design is assembled. It is surprising how different it can look when it is reduced to the smaller pieces of the design from the larger pieces of fabric at the start.

### CONSTRUCTION
#### *Making the Hexagon Template*

The hexagon is based on a 120° angle in each corner of the six-sided shape. This is a complex geometric exercise to draw and usually quilters just buy a template in whatever size they can get. However, drawing a hexagon in any size you want is easy if you use isometric paper. This is a type of graph paper printed with lines arranged to make

equilateral triangles each with a corner angle of 60°. By drawing along these lines it is a simple matter to draft triangles and hexagons of any size (Fig 2).

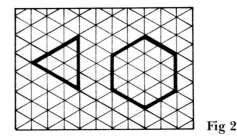

**Fig 2**

The size of hexagon I have chosen for the block is in a suitable scale for this design. If I were to make a larger piece in the design I am sure I would use a larger hexagon. When in doubt, cut out some hexagons from isometric paper and play with them before making a decision.

**1** Make the template by tracing the hexagon shape from Fig 3, cutting it out and sticking it on to card, or use template plastic. See page 9 for instructions on making templates.

**2** This design will keep its position efficiently if the papers are cut from freezer paper rather than from thick paper. If freezer paper is not available, the outer wrapping from packs of photocopying paper is an excellent substitute. Using a really sharp pencil to keep the shape accurate, draw round the template on the non-shiny side of the freezer paper. Mark the corners of the hexagons by continuing the drawn lines to just beyond the template corners so they cross (Fig 4). This cross marks the exact corner and will make cutting out more accurate.

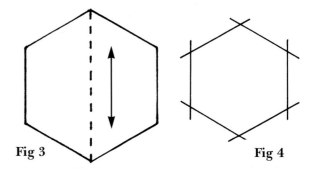

**Fig 3**　　　　　　　　　　　　　　**Fig 4**

**3** Cut out forty-two freezer paper hexagons, cutting just inside the drawn lines to prevent the shape becoming larger than the original hexagon template.

**4** From the three fabrics chosen for the design cut two strips of each colour, each measuring 1¹/₄in (3.2cm) wide and 30in (70cm) long. Stitch these together in pairs as shown in Fig 5, stitching a 1/4in (6mm) wide seam. Use a much smaller machine stitch than usual to discourage the seams from coming undone when cut. Press the seams open after stitching.

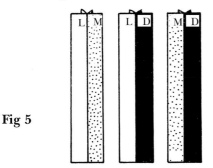

**Fig 5**

**5** Place one joined strip right side down on an ironing pad. Position a freezer paper hexagon shiny side down on the fabric as shown in Fig 6 and press with a dry iron using a wool setting. This will fix the paper in exactly the right position and prevent it from shifting while the fabric is stitched over the paper. Position and press thirteen more hexagon papers on to the reverse of the joined strips leaving 1/2in (1.2cm) between each paper as shown in Fig 7.

Repeat this with the other two joined strips, positioning fourteen hexagons on each piece.

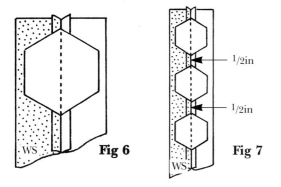

**Fig 6**     **Fig 7**

**6** Cut around each paper, adding a 1/4in (6mm) seam allowance on all sides. This does not have to be carefully measured as it is not critical. However, try to avoid cutting a seam allowance less than 1/4in (6mm) as this makes tacking difficult.

**7** Thread a needle with tacking thread (I use either crewel needles or sharps 8 or 9). Begin with a knot and tack fabric to paper by folding the fabric tightly over the paper and stitching it down. Take care when turning the corners that include the joining seam that the fabric strips do not pull the machine stitches undone as you turn the fabric over the paper. Finish with a backstitch and cut

the thread leaving about 1/4in (6mm) for security (Fig 8). Turn the tacked shape over and check that the corners exactly outline the shape of the paper hexagon beneath it (Fig 9).

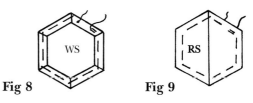

**Fig 8**     **Fig 9**

**8** Arrange one hexagon from each joined strip in the desired design (Fig 10). Each group of three hexagons is joined in exactly the same arrangement of light, medium and dark fabrics. There will be fourteen Y-shaped units altogether. Thread a needle with no more than 18in (45.7cm) of toning thread. If stitching two different coloured fabrics together match the thread to the darker fabric as it is always less obvious than the lighter.

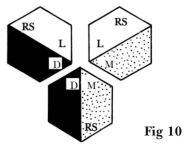

**Fig 10**

Take two hexagon shapes and place them right sides together, ready to sew. If one edge seems longer than the other, (this happens more often than you would think, so do not blame yourself), place them with the shorter edge on top as you work. As you sew, the top layer stretches, just as it does on a sewing machine, so you can ease the shorter edge to fit the longer. Fix the corner you are working towards with a pin (Fig 11) so that as you stitch the two corners will match exactly.

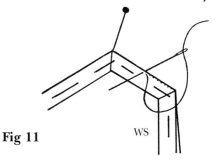

**Fig 11**     WS

**9** Starting with a double stitch to secure the thread, oversew with small even stitches, making sure that both sets of corners match exactly.

PAM PUTTICK

*'I dedicated this quilt to my husband for his patience and understanding*
*now that I have become a quilting fiend.'*

The stitches should be about the same distance apart as small machine stitches. If you stitch too closely you can weaken the fabric and make an almost satin stitch effect which will prevent the finished seam from lying flat. Finish the seam with a double stitch and cut the thread, leaving about 1/4in (6mm) for safety.

**10** Open out the two joined hexagons and attach the third hexagon in the same way, stitching a double stitch at the centre of all three to strengthen the centre (Fig 12).

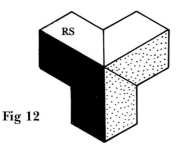

**Fig 12**

**11** Assemble all fourteen Y-shaped units in the same way and join them together in rows as in Fig 13. Join the rows together to make the final design as in Fig 14.

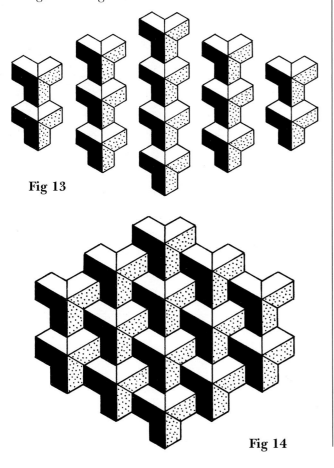

**Fig 13**

**Fig 14**

**12** Press before removing the freezer papers so outer seam allowances remain turned under. Remove the tacking by undoing the final stitch, pulling firmly on the knot to pull the thread out in one length. Pull the papers off the fabric. Tack around the outer edges of the design to keep the seam allowances in place.

**13** Cut a 13 1/2 x 13 1/2in (34.3 x 34.3cm) square of fabric for the background. This can be trimmed after the design is stitched in position to whatever size seems best, probably 13 x 13in (33 x 33cm). When one fabric is stitched to another (known as appliqué) the bottom fabric often draws up slightly to finish up smaller than when you started. By using a 13 1/2 x 13 1/2in (34.3 x 34.3cm) square it can be accurately trimmed to 13in (33cm) once the design has been stitched in place.

**14** Place the Inner City design centrally on the background. It helps to fold the square in half from top to bottom and crease lightly. The crease makes a central guideline for positioning the design. Pin or tack the Inner City on to the background square. Using a shade of thread to match the design not the background, sew it on to the background, keeping stitches small and even. Sew a double stitch at each corner to secure it (Fig 15). Be prepared to change the colour of the thread to match each fabric as you stitch around the design.

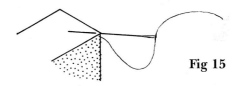

**Fig 15**

**15** Before an appliquéd shape is quilted, its thickness can be reduced by cutting the background fabric away from behind the appliqué. This is not compulsory and if you are nervous about doing this, leave it. However, it does make the whole piece easier to quilt and allows it to lie flatter. Turn the block to the back and, with your fingers, just pull the backing from the appliqué at the centre. Make a small cut in the backing fabric about 1/4–1/2in (6–12mm) inside the line of stitches. Once you have done this, carefully cut away the backing up to 1/4in (6mm) from the stitching line of the appliqué, leaving the appliqué itself intact.

**16** Trim the finished block to an exact 13in (33cm) square, or to whatever size you feel suits your design. Add the inner framing strips and trim the block to exactly 14in (35.6cm) square. Finally, add the sashing strips (see page 130).

# SEMINOLE

This attractive form of strip patchwork was begun by the Seminole Native Americans in Florida around the beginning of the century. They used plain fabrics in glowing colours to create variations of border designs to use in their blouses, jackets and skirts. It was never a hand technique: the Seminole women used hand sewing machines for their complex designs. Now we can use modern machines plus fast and accurate rotary cutting equipment for our own versions of Seminole work.

## COLOUR CHOICES

Two variations of Seminole patchwork are used in the block in the Sampler Quilt (Fig 1). The centre band is of the classic squares-on-point design and uses three fabrics. The outer two bands are from the same zig-zag chevron pattern and use two fabrics alternating in the centre with a third on either side. It would keep the design clearer to use the same three fabrics for each variation. Once these are made, they can be arranged in the block and a decision can then be made about the dividing fabric strips which also border the block.

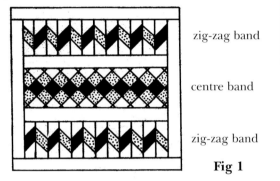

zig-zag band

centre band

zig-zag band

**Fig 1**

There needs to be some definition between the two fabrics that are used together in the centre of each design band. The third fabric becomes an edging background to the other two, so if you are using certain fabrics throughout as background, these might be suitable here. Take the fabrics and lay them out in order to check that you like the relationship between them – you may want to swap one over with another or even reject one at this stage.

## CONSTRUCTION
### The Centre Seminole Band

**1** Having decided on the position of each fabric in the design refer to Fig 2 and cut from fabric A (centre) one strip 1¹/₂in (3.8cm) wide and 16in (40.6cm) long. Cut from fabric B two strips 1¹/₂in (3.8cm) wide and 16in (40.6cm) long. Cut from fabric C two strips 1³/₄in (4.5cm) wide and 16in (40.6cm) long. Notice that the strips that are on the *outside* edges of the band are cut ¹/₄in (6mm) wider than the others.

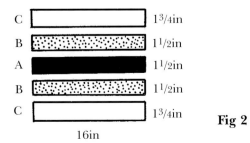

| C | | 1³/₄in |
| B | | 1¹/₂in |
| A | | 1¹/₂in |
| B | | 1¹/₂in |
| C | | 1³/₄in |

16in

**Fig 2**

**2** Set the stitch length on your sewing machine to about two-thirds the size of the usual dressmaking stitch to prevent the seam from coming undone when the strips are cut across. Choose a thread colour that will not strongly contrast with any of your fabrics, darker rather than lighter. I find that shades of grey or neutral will blend in with most fabric combinations. The seams need to be a scant ¹/₄in (6mm). Use a ¹/₄in (6mm) foot or a strip of masking tape on the machine to help you stitch an accurate seam. Stitch the five strips together, alternating the direction you sew the strips to keep the band straight and not slightly rippled (Fig 3).

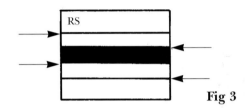

RS

**Fig 3**

**3** Press the band of strips from the *front* with the seams pressed in the same direction.

**4** Take the band and place it horizontally on the cutting board, lining up the top edge with one of the horizontal markings on the board. Place the band with the seams pressed towards the top of the band as this will make it easier to cut. If the band is slightly rippled, do not worry, just pat it as flat as you can and carry on. If five strips of different fabrics lie perfectly flat, this is a miracle.

Using a rotary ruler and cutter, trim one end of the band vertically to straighten it and then cut off a piece 1¹/₂in (3.8cm) wide (Fig 4). Continue to cut off similar pieces each 1¹/₂in (3.8cm) wide. You should get ten pieces from the band of strips.

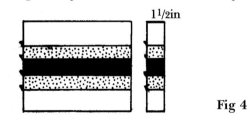

1¹/₂in

**Fig 4**

**5** Place the ten pieces ready for stitching next to the sewing machine. Take two pieces, place them next to each other, then turn the right hand piece round 180° so that the seams are now lying in the opposite direction to those of the first piece. This will make it easier to match the seams. Step the second piece *down* so that the seams line up as shown in Fig 5, page 21. Flip piece 2 over onto piece 1, right sides facing, and pin the first seam alignment.

### HEATHER JACKSON

*'Having decided to use a very limited palette of five plain fabrics, my choice for each block was easy – no choice at all! Halfway through I added the green to make up the number for the Bargello design and this proved invaluable in several of the other blocks.'*

Pin diagonally, as this will help to keep both sets of seam allowances flat while stitching (Fig 6).

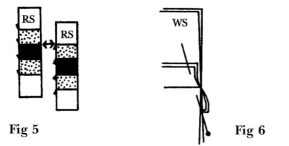

**Fig 5**                                                **Fig 6**

If it worries you to let the other seams lock in naturally as you stitch without pinning them, then pin all three seam junctions before stitching – I stitch as far as the pin at the first seam junction, remove the pin and before continuing to stitch, lock the next set of seams together with a stitch ripper and hold them firmly in place as I stitch. I repeat this for each of the seam junctions as I get to them. If this works for you, don't bother to pin excessively. If you have cut and stitched your strips together accurately, there shouldn't be a problem. If there *is* a problem, blame the fabric and pin each seam junction before stitching.

**6** Open out the two joined pieces and check that the positioning is correct. Pick up piece 3 and turn it so that the pressed seams are lying in the opposite direction to piece 2. Step piece 3 down in the same way as before. Flip it over onto piece 2 and match and pin the first seam alignment. Stitch, matching the three seam junctions carefully either by holding them in place or by pinning. Open the pieces out and check that all is well. If you spot a poorly matched seam junction, leave it until all ten pieces are joined. You may well be able to cut the band of pieces here and so lose the nasty bit. Repeat the process with piece 4, then 5 and so on until all ten pieces are joined.

### Chain Stitching

You can save time and thread by stitching the pieces together with chain sewing – stitching each pair together one after the other without taking them off the machine and breaking the thread. If you do this, remember that each pair of pieces must be arranged identically with pressed seams in exactly the same direction each time.

To chain sew, stitch to the very end of the first pair and, without lifting the pressure foot, place the next pair in position and continue to stitch, starting at the top edge of the pieces (Fig 7). Continue to chain sew the pairs until all are joined.

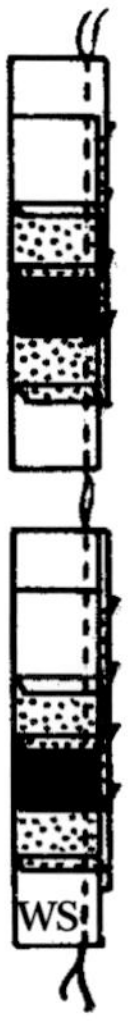

Take them off the machine and cut the threads that hold each pair to the next.

Open out two pairs, line up the seams, pin and stitch them together, chaining the second set after them. (The remaining pair has to sit this round out.) Finally, join together the three sections, lining up the seams as before.

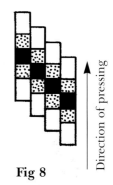

**7** Press the band from the front, pushing the seams to one side. Use your hand to guide the seams towards one side and try to press each strip from bottom to **Fig 7** top along the grain of the fabric rather than across the band, as this can stretch and distort the band (Fig 8).

**Fig 8**

**8** At this stage the band of pieces needs to be straightened up at either end (Fig 9). It would, however, be very wasteful to cut off the excess from both ends. There is a cunning way to straighten the band without any waste. Study the band and choose a part where you are not too happy with the matching of the seams. Place the band horizontally on a cutting board, positioning the top points along a horizontal marking on the board (Fig 10). Place a rotary ruler vertically on the band at the point where you are unhappy with the seam-matching. This cannot be near either

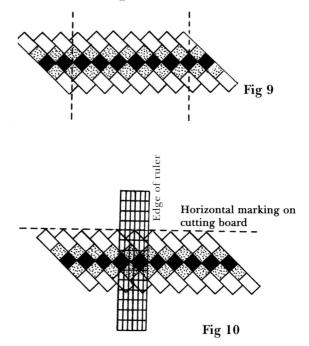

**Fig 9**

Horizontal marking on cutting board

**Fig 10**

end, but anywhere along the band is fine. Position the ruler through the centre of a diamond to keep the design balanced. Cut through the design with a rotary cutter – not a nice moment, but be brave. Remove the left-hand section and place it at the other end of the right hand section (Fig 11). Step the design downwards to match the other pieces. Match the seams as before and stitch the two sections together. Press this last seam from the front to one side in the same direction as the other seams. Your band is now straight!

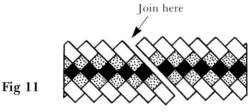

**Fig 11**

**9** It is also very stretchy if you pull it from side to side, so edging strips must be attached to keep it firm. It is probably best to leave this until all three bands of Seminole have been completed before choosing which fabric looks best for the strips.

### Making the Zig-Zag Bands

**10** I used the same set of three fabrics for this design as for the centre band, which helps to unify the overall design. Using the zig-zag design in two short lengths in this block is quite wasteful as a triangular wedge at each end of the strips is cut off and discarded. However, it is a lovely design and if used in longer lengths as a quilt border would not be wasteful at all.

Cut two sets of strips as in Fig 12, each 1½in (3.8cm) wide and 31in (78.7cm) long. Stitch these together into two bands. Press seams from the front with the seams pressed all in one direction.

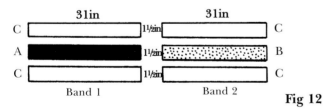

**Fig 12**

**11** Take band 1 and place it horizontally on the cutting board right side *up*. Take band 2 and place it right side *down*, on top of band 1 with the seams lying in the opposite direction to band 1 (Fig 13). Match the edges and seams carefully.

The pieces for the zig-zag design are cut at an angle of 45° to the strips. This is easy to do with a

rotary ruler using the 45° marked line. Look carefully at your ruler: some are a mass of criss-crossed extra lines, but one or

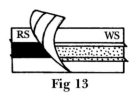

**Fig 13**

more will be labelled 45°. Place the ruler across the bands of fabric with the 45° line running along the top edges of the fabric as shown in Fig 14. If you can't seem to match your ruler with the diagrams, try another 45° line on the ruler or flip the ruler over and use the wrong side of the 45° line. Cut through both layers of fabric with a rotary cutter along the angled edge of the ruler (Fig 15). Remove the two triangles of fabric.

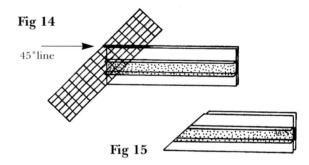

**Fig 14**

**Fig 15**

**12** Find the marking on the ruler that is 1½in (3.8cm) from one long edge. Pass the ruler over the slanted cut edges of the fabric until the 1½in (3.8cm) line is exactly on top of the cut edges (Fig 16). Cut along the ruler's edge with a rotary cutter. Lift the ruler and set aside the pair of cut pieces. Repeat the process, cutting a total of twelve pairs of pieces.

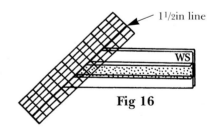

**Fig 16**

**13** Open out the first pair – it should look like Fig 17. Close the pair together again with right sides facing and pin the edges carefully, matching the seams. Stitch this first pair together. Continue to pin and stitch each pair in exactly the same arrangement as the first. This can very easily be done using the chain sewing technique described earlier. Open each zig-zag out and press from the front with the seams to one side.

**Fig 17**

**14** Join six zig-zags together, pinning and matching seams carefully (Fig 18). Chain sew if possible as it saves so much time and thread. This makes the top band for the block. Join the remaining six zig-zags for the bottom band. Press from the front with seams pressed all in one direction.

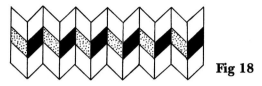

**Fig 18**

### Attaching the Edging Strips

**15** Arrange the three Seminole bands as shown in Fig 1 (page 19) so that you can choose the fabric that will look best between the bands. I used the same fabric to border the block, but this may not be your choice. At this stage your three bands will not be the same length – probably the centre band will be longer than the two zig-zag bands. Trim down the centre band equally from both ends to match the zig-zag bands. If the zig-zag bands are not exactly the same length as each other, press and ease out the shorter band with a steam iron until it matches the longer band. When you have either cut or stretched the bands so that they are all the same length, cut two strips of the edging fabric each 1¹/₂in (3.8cm) wide and a length to match the Seminole bands.

**16** Place the centre Seminole band horizontally on the cutting board and lay a rotary ruler along the inner seam lines (Fig 19). The band is very flexible and you can move parts of it up and down so that as many inner points as possible can be lined up with the edge of the ruler. Don't expect miracles – not all the inner points will be exactly on line, just get as many as possible. Ignore seam allowances that may be showing – it is where the actual stitch lines end that you are lining up the ruler (Fig 20). Draw along the edge of the ruler with a soft marking pencil.

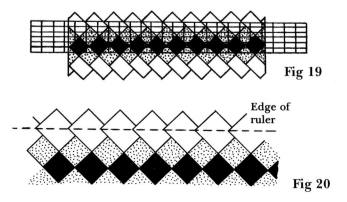

**Fig 19**

Edge of ruler

**Fig 20**

**17** Turn the centre Seminole band through 180° and repeat the process. While doing this check that both drawn lines are parallel to each other so that the width of the finished band will be consistent.

**18** Place one edging strip right side *down* on the Seminole band, matching its edge with a drawn line on the band (Fig 21). Pin it in position and stitch with the usual ¹/₄in (6mm) seam. Repeat this with the second strip, pinning it along the second drawn line and stitching it in position.

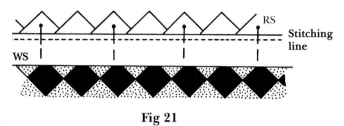

RS

Stitching line

WS

**Fig 21**

Press back the strips and check that the section of Seminole design is looking evenly balanced between the strips. Once you are happy with it, trim the pointed sections back to within ¹/₄in (6mm) of the seamline.

**19** Place one zig-zag band horizontally on the cutting board. Place a rotary ruler across the band and align the top points of each inner zig-zag as much as possible with the line on the ruler that is ¹/₂in (12mm) from its edge (Fig 22). Cut along the edge of the ruler with a rotary cutter. Repeat this at the other end of the zig-zag band. Trim the second zig-zag band in the same way.

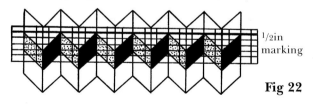

¹/₂in marking

**Fig 22**

**20** Pin and stitch each zig-zag band to either side of the centre design, taking care not to stretch the zig-zag band while stitching it. Press the seams from the front towards the edging strips.

**21** Measure the block from top to bottom and from side to side. Trim down wherever necessary to make it square, or just add wider border strips on the shorter sides. The block needs to finish up exactly 14in (35.6cm) square once the framing strips are added. If the block measures 11in (29.2cm) or more, cut the border strips 2in (5cm) wide and trim the block down afterwards to 14in (35.6cm) square. Finally, add the sashing strips (see page 130).

# TANGLED STAR

I first saw this traditional pattern in a calendar designed by an American quilter friend Pepper Cory. Each month featured a different design, all based on stars and all measuring 12in (30.5cm) square. The twelve squares, known as blocks, were combined in a quilt in much the same way as my Sampler Quilt. I particularly like this block because of the way the interlocking shapes weave over and under each other.

The traditional way to make a patchwork block

like this is to draw it out onto graph paper and make templates of the various shapes that make up the design. No seam allowances are included. This is the way that the patchwork blocks that evolved over the years in the United States have all been made: new designs were drawn out, stuck onto card and then cut into the required templates. The templates were drawn around on the back of the chosen fabrics and the shapes cut out with a seam allowance added to the drawn lines. With intricate designs like this the old way still seems to be the best. It is quite possible for the ace machinists to piece this block by machine, following the drawn lines with machine stitches instead of by hand. However, there are some nasty angles in the design which can present problems to the less experienced machinist so I suggest this block is pieced by hand.

## COLOUR CHOICES

The essence of the design is a spiky star and a square shape that weave through each other on a background (Fig 1). The tangled shapes are not stitched on to a large background square but every piece is cut to shape and joined with its neighbour to form the complete block. The two fabrics for the star and square need to look good together with the third background fabric. Try folding the fabrics into small shapes and arranging them side by side on the possible background fabric when choosing. An extra colour could be used in the central area to give more depth if desired. You may be planning to use a certain fabric throughout the quilt as the background, in which case your choice of fabrics for the star and square shapes will be controlled by this. Remember that the block will finish up a 12in (30.5cm) square and will need a framing border before the sashing strips, so this extra fabric should also be considered when choices are being made.

## CONSTRUCTION

1 Make card templates by tracing the six shapes from Fig 2 (page 26), cutting them out and sticking them on the card, or use template plastic. Mark the directional arrows as these show how the template should be positioned on the grain or weave of the fabric. Mark the centre corner on template B. When the four quarters of the design have been assembled, this corner of each of the four sections is positioned in the centre of the block.

2 On the wrong side of each fabric draw around the templates accurately using a sharp marking pencil and matching the direction of the arrows

with the grain of the fabric. The drawn lines mark the sewing lines. Allow at least 1/2in (1.2cm) between each drawn outline so that the seam allowances of 1/4in (6mm) can be added to the shape when cutting out.

For the larger star shape you will need four of shape A, four of shape D and four of shape E. For the smaller square shape you will need four of shape C and four of shape A *reversed* on the fabric. To do this, flip the template over on the fabric making sure that the grain-line arrow matches the weave of the fabric.

For the background you will need four of shape B (the centre background shape), four of shape F and four of shape F *reversed*.

3 Cut out each shape to include the 1/4in (6mm) seam allowance, either by eye or by using a rotary cutter and ruler. The seam allowance is not critical, but it is very helpful if cut accurately as then the edges of the fabrics line up as you match the drawn stitching lines.

4 Arrange the cut pieces on a flat surface or pin them in position on a polystyrene tile or board. Final decisions can be made on the effectiveness of the fabric choices at this stage.

5 This design breaks into four quarters, each identical in design and construction (Fig 3a). Any block that divides in this way is called a Four-Patch. Assemble each quarter in turn as shown in Fig 3b before joining them all together.

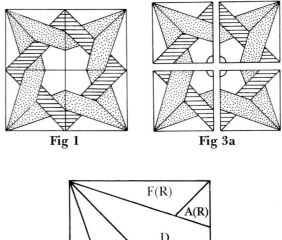

**Fig 1**          **Fig 3a**

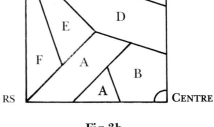

**Fig 3b**

25

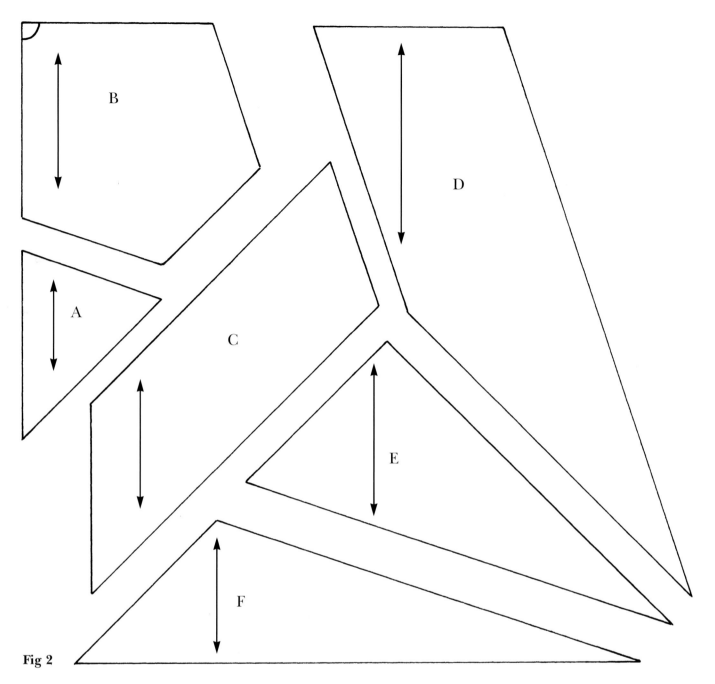

**Fig 2**

The order of joining (known as piecing) each quarter section is not immediately obvious. First join piece A to piece B and then attach C (Fig 4).

Work with the *right* side of the fabric uppermost when first arranging the pieces as this gives the design shown in Fig 3b: from the back of the fabric the design is reversed, which can be confusing.

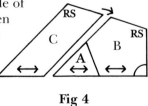

**Fig 4**

Place shapes A and B with right sides facing along the two sides to be joined. The pencil marks will be on the outside and must be positioned exactly on top of each other as they indicate the sewing lines. Align the starting point of the sewing lines by pushing a pin through both layers of fabric until the head is on the surface of the top fabric. Repeat this to mark the finishing point (Fig 5). Reposition the pins at right angles to the seam. Add more pins along the seamline, matching the marked lines (Fig 6).

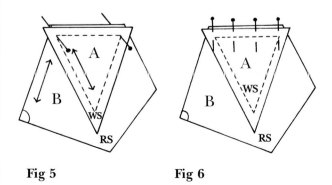

**Fig 5**　　　　　**Fig 6**

### Kate Badrick

*'Someone commented that this quilt "glows" and I think it does.*
*I attribute this to the inspiration, discussion and general enthusiasm that*
*emanated from Lynne and the other members of the class. For me, it represents*
*the great pleasure and fun that went into its production.'*

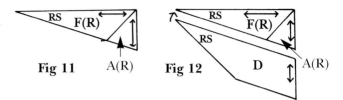

**Fig 11**     A(R)        **Fig 12**        D        A(R)

**6** Starting with a double stitch, sew along the pencilled line with small running stitches about the same length as machine stitches, loading several stitches on to the needle at a time. Begin each run of stitches with a backstitch to secure the work firmly (Fig 7). Do not sew into the seam allowances, these are left free so that once the block is complete the seams may be pressed to one side. They are never pressed open, as the hand-sewn stitches are not strong enough. Do not press any seams until the whole piece is complete as there is no set rule for which way each seam is to be pressed – just wait until the block is assembled and then press the seams whichever way avoids too much bulk at the back of the work.

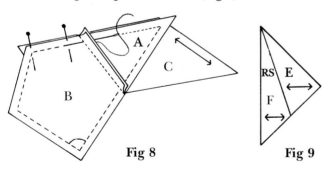

**Fig 7**

**7** Once piece A is joined to B, pin piece C in place onto A and B with right sides facing. When stitching this second seam don't sew over the seam allowances in the middle. Instead, sew up to the seam and make a backstitch. Pass the needle through the seam allowances to the other side. Backstitch again and continue sewing (Fig 8). In the same way pin and stitch together pieces E and F (Fig 9).

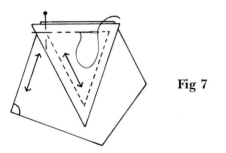

**Fig 8**          **Fig 9**

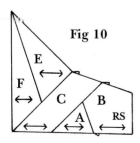

**Fig 10**

**8** Join together the first section (A + B + C) and the second section (E + F) as in Fig 10.
**9** Pin and stitch together pieces A (reversed) and F (reversed) as in Fig 11. Pin and stitch piece D to this pair as in Fig 12.

**10** Finally, join the two parts of the design together to complete it. Take care to match the stitching lines exactly, especially at the centre of the design where the shape D makes a wide angle. This is the part that is so much easier to negotiate by hand rather than by machine. As before, stitch to the junction of seams, make a backstitch to secure it, pass the needle through the seam allowances and make another backstitch before continuing stitching along the seamline. This completed square forms one quarter of the block.
**11** Pin and stitch the other three quarters of the block in the same way. Arrange the four sections in the block design (see Fig 1). Stitch the top two sections together, pinning and stitching along the drawn lines as before. Repeat this with the remaining two sections (Fig 13). Finally, stitch the two halves together, matching the centres carefully.

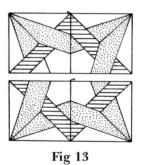

**Fig 13**

**12** Press the completed block lightly, pushing the seams in whichever direction reduces the bulk of the seam allowances. The block should measure 12½ x 12½in (31.7 x 31.7cm). This is a 12in (30.5cm) square block but the extra ¼in (6mm) seam allowances on both sides make it up to 12½in (31.7cm) at this stage.
**13** Check that your block measures exactly 12½in (31.7cm) in both directions. If it is slightly smaller, add ¼in (6mm) to the width of the framing strips and after these are added to the block trim the whole thing down to exactly 14in (35.6cm) square. If the block measures more than 12½in (31.7cm) square, add the framing strips and then trim all the sides down to the final measurement of 14in (35.6cm) square. Finally, add the sashing strips (see page 130).

# QUICK TRIANGLES

In the first *Sampler Quilt Book* I included a block that was based on sixteen squares, each of which was divided diagonally into two halves (Fig 2). Traditionally these were constructed by drawing round a template, cutting out the shapes to include a ¼in (6mm) seam allowance and then piecing them together by hand or machine, following the drawn sewing lines in the American piecing

technique. There is a quicker and easier way of mass-producing these squares already pieced, using rotary cutting equipment and a sewing machine. You will still have to join the squares together and match the corners accurately but the preliminary cutting and stitching is simplified.

Fig 1

The block for this new quilt (Fig 1) combines eight squares that are divided into two triangles and eight squares divided into four triangles (Fig 3). The technique for making each set of squares is similar but different measurements must be used for each set.

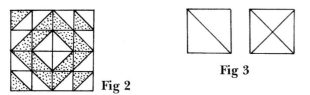

Fig 2

Fig 3

When making half-square triangles for a machined design that uses 3in (7.6cm) squares finished size, an extra 1/2in (1.2cm) must be added for the seam allowances on either side plus another 3/8in (1cm) to allow for the diagonal seam across the square, making 7/8in (2.2cm) in total. In other words, for a finished 3in (7.6cm) square the starting measurement must be 37/8in (9.8cm) (Fig 4). The same 7/8in (2.2cm) is always added to any size finished square when using this technique to make half-square triangles.

When making quarter-square triangles there are extra seam allowances to be included in the calcu-

lations. In addition to the usual 1/2in (1.2cm) for the seam allowances on each side there are two diagonal seams across the square. All these seams mean that a total of 11/4in (3.2cm) needs to be added to the finished measurement of the square. So for a 3in (7.6cm) finished square, the starting measurement must be 41/4in (10.8cm) (Fig 5).

To construct quarter-square triangles using any size finished square, 11/4in (3.2cm) must always be added to the finished square measurement. These are not easy measurements to play with, but need to be used to produce an accurate set of squares.

## COLOUR CHOICES

The design of triangles shown in Fig 1 uses four fabrics, two combined for the half-square triangles and two more for the quarter-square triangles. In my block I used two very similar cream fabrics with two similar blue fabrics, but you may like to introduce a wider range of shades. The half-square triangles make a large diamond in the centre of the block and also appear as corners, so the strongest of your fabrics may look best here teamed with a background fabric. Once the sixteen squares have been constructed it is possible to play with them and use an arrangement that is different from the one shown in Fig 1 if it suits your fabric better.

## CONSTRUCTION
### Making the Half-square Triangles

1 From each of the two chosen fabrics cut a piece measuring about 81/2 x 81/2in (21.6 x 21.6cm). Place them right sides together and press. This will help keep the two layers in place. It greatly helps the precision piecing of the fabrics if they are spray-starched before use, particularly the fabric for the quarter-square triangles. This keeps everything firm while stitching, especially the stretchy bias edges and corners.

2 Place the two layers of fabric on a cutting board. On the top fabric you are going to draw a grid of four squares – two rows of two – each square measuring 37/8in (9.8cm) (Fig 6). To do this accurately it is better to use the measurements on the ruler rather than those on the cutting board. Find the line of marks on the ruler that are 37/8in

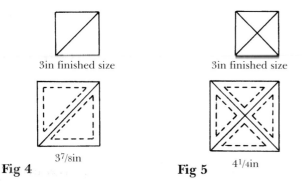

3in finished size

3in finished size

37/8in

41/4in

Fig 4

Fig 5

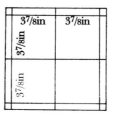

Fig 6

(9.8cm) from one edge. You may find it easier to mark this distance by sticking a small piece of tape at each end of the ruler on the 3$^7$/8in (9.8cm) line. Place the ruler vertically about 1/4in (6mm) from the left-hand edge of the fabrics (Fig 7a).

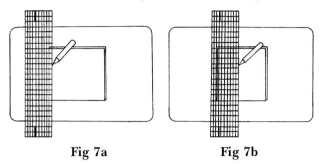

**Fig 7a**         **Fig 7b**

Using a marking pencil, draw a line from top to bottom on the fabric along the ruler's edge. Move the ruler across the fabric to the right until the marked 3$^7$/8in (9.8cm) line is exactly on top of the drawn line (Fig 7b). Draw a line along the ruler's edge. Once again move the ruler across to the right until the new drawn line lies exactly under the 3$^7$/8in (9.8cm) line on the ruler. Draw a line along the ruler's edge. Left-handed quilters should begin marking from the right-hand side and move the ruler across the fabric to the left.

**3** Turn the ruler horizontally and draw a line on the fabric about 1/4in (6mm) from the bottom edges (Fig 8a). As before, move the ruler upwards over the fabric until the 3$^7$/8in (9.8cm) line is exactly on top of the drawn line (Fig 8b). Draw a line along the ruler's edge. Repeat this once more to complete the grid of two rows of two squares each.

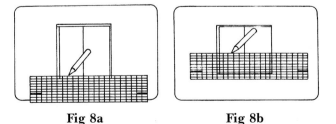

**Fig 8a**         **Fig 8b**

**4** Draw diagonal lines across each square in one direction only, as shown in Fig 9.
**5** Pin the two fabrics together with four to six pins to hold the layers while stitching.
**6** Machine a line of stitching on *either side* of the drawn diagonal lines at exactly 1/4in (6mm) using a slightly smaller stitch than usual (Fig 10). If you have a strip of masking tape stuck to your machine as a stitching guide you will not be able to see it

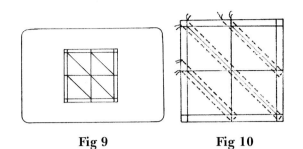

**Fig 9**         **Fig 10**

through the layers of fabric, so another way of stitching accurately must be found, such as:
a) use a special 1/4in (6mm) foot on the machine;
b) if your machine has the facility, move the needle until the distance between it and the side of your usual machine foot is exactly 1/4in (6mm);
c) draw in a stitching line 1/4in (6mm) away from the diagonal line on both sides, using a different colour marking pencil to avoid confusion.
**7** Once the pairs of lines have been stitched, take the fabrics from the machine and place them on the cutting board. Remove the pins and using a ruler and cutter, cut along the drawn vertical lines. Without moving the fabric, cut along the drawn horizontal lines. Finally, cut along the drawn diagonal lines (Fig 11). You will find that a miracle has happened and that when you pick up each triangle of fabric it has been stitched to another and you have a pieced square made of two triangles of two different fabrics. Some of the triangles will have a line of stitches across one cor-ner (Fig 12). Loosen these gently by pulling the fabrics apart – they will easily come undone and the threads can be removed.
**8** Press each square from the front with the seams towards the darker colour.

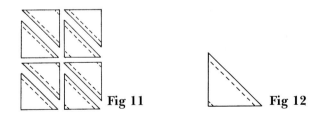

**Fig 11**         **Fig 12**

### Making the Quarter-square Triangles
**9** From each of the two chosen fabrics cut a piece measuring 9 x 9in (22.8 x 22.8cm). Place them right sides together and press.
**10** Place the two layers of fabric on a cutting board and draw a grid of four squares as before, but this time each square must be 4$^1$/4 x 4$^1$/4in (10.8 x 10.8cm). You may not need to mark your ruler with tape as it is easier to find the 4$^1$/4in (10.8cm) line than it was the 3$^7$/8in (9.8cm) line (Fig 13, page 33).

GILL SHEPHERD

*'I fell for the William Morris fabrics and managed to find co-ordinating browns and a yellow that brought the patterns to life. I wanted to do "my own thing" for the border and am really pleased with the finished quilt.'*

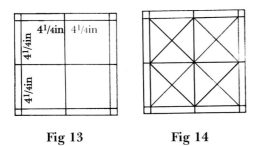

**Fig 13**

**Fig 14**

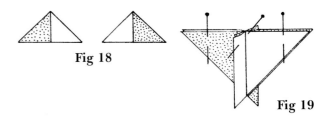

**Fig 18**

**Fig 19**

**11** Draw diagonal lines across each square in *both* directions, as shown in Fig 14.

**12** Pin the layers together with four to six pins and machine a line of stitching on either side of *one* set of diagonal lines at a distance of ¼in (6mm) from the line. Leave the other set of diagonal lines unstitched (Fig 15).

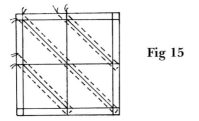

**Fig 15**

**13** Place the fabrics on the cutting board and remove the pins. Using a rotary ruler and cutter, cut along all the drawn vertical lines. Without moving the fabric, cut along the drawn horizontal lines. Take each square and first cut along the *unstitched* drawn diagonal lines (Fig 16). Then cut the drawn lines between the stitched lines (Fig 17).

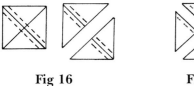

**Fig 16**

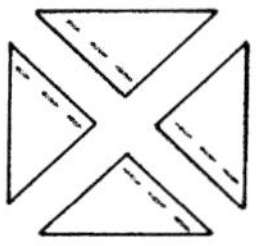

**Fig 17**

**14** Open out each shape, easing apart any stitched corners. Press the seams towards the darker fabric.

**15** The pieced triangles will be in two different arrangements (Fig 18). Separate them into two piles, one for each arrangement. Using one pile only, match the triangular shapes into pairs to make squares. Place them right sides facing and pin the centre matching seams carefully. I pin diagonally so that the seam allowances stay flat while stitching (Fig 19). It is better not to pin the sharp corners together, as these can stretch and get munched up by the machine. The seam you are going to stitch is a stretchy bias diagonal, so handle the fabrics as little as possible. If you have

spray-starched your fabric it will be much firmer and easier to handle. Don't starch now, as the fabrics will distort and even shrink as you iron them dry. Just remember to try it next time round. . . Match and pin the second set of triangular shapes to make squares in the same way.

**16** Stitch the pairs together, guiding them through the machine with the point of a stitch-ripper or small pair of scissors. Press the seams to one side, pressing from the front of the work.

**17** Arrange the sixteen pieced squares in the design shown in Fig 1 or try another arrangement if you prefer it. If all the squares do not fit together perfectly, remember that you can swap the squares around as there are eight identical pieces in each set to play with.

**18** Sew together the top four squares to make a row. There are several places where two triangles meet in a point. Where this occurs, check that once they are joined the two triangles meet in an arrowhead ¼in (6mm) from the top edges of the fabric (Fig 20). From the front, press all seams on row one in the same direction.

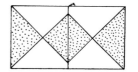

**Fig 20**

**19** Join together the four squares in row two. From the front press the seams in the opposite direction to row one. Join rows one and two, matching seams carefully, especially where two arrowheads meet. Position the tips of the arrowheads exactly on top of each other, checking by peeling the top fabrics back with the pin. When the arrowheads meet, hold them in position firmly and pin. I use long, extra-fine pins so that I can machine-stitch over them if necessary. Stitch the seam. Join row three and add it to row two in the same way. Finally, join and add row four to complete the block. Press the block from the front.

**20** Add the inner framing strips and trim the block to an exact 14in (35.6cm) square, then add the sashing strips. See page 130 for adding framing strips and sashing.

# CELTIC KNOT

This particular area of patchwork emerged in the early 1980s with the work of Philomena Durcan, a quilter originally from Southern Ireland who was then living in California. She adapted the principle of stained glass patchwork to the Celtic designs of her homeland, using bias strips as the traditional Celtic strapping.

All Celtic designs are based on complex interwoven bands, each winding over and under each other, all seemingly without end. The medallion

design used in the Celtic Knot patchwork block in this New Sampler Quilt shows all these characteristics. Constructing the block requires a 1/4in (6mm) bias bar, a tool useful for producing the narrow strips needed for Celtic work.

### COLOUR CHOICES

The Celtic Knot is a central design placed on a background (Fig 1). One fabric is used for the base of the medallion, with the option of a second used in the centre space (not shown in Fig 1). All the lines of the Celtic Knot strapping are made from bias strips which are pinned and stitched onto the medallion fabric. Don't be afraid to use patterned or even striped fabric for the bias strips, as it adds greatly to the richness of the design. If you are doubtful, cut one bias strip of the proposed fabric and lay it across the medallion fabric to get an idea of how they look together.

**Fig 1**

### CONSTRUCTION

**1** The design drawn in Fig 2 (page 36) is half the Celtic Knot. Trace it on to a large piece of tracing paper, including the centre dotted line. Rotate the tracing paper 180° and complete the Knot by tracing the other part of the design, matching the centre dotted lines.

**2** From the medallion fabric cut a square 11 x 11in (27.9 x 27.9cm). The Knot design must be transferred to the *front* of this square of fabric. Place the fabric over the traced design, matching the grain-line arrows on the drawing with the straight grain of the fabric (the direction of the woven threads). Trace it on to the fabric with a sharp marking pencil – use a light box if necessary or dressmaker's carbon paper. Do not trace the dotted centre line on to the fabric. Simplify the double lines of the design by drawing only *one* line midway between the two parallel lines. The over-and-under arrangement can be shown by leaving a gap in the drawn line when it should lie *underneath* a crossing line (Fig 3). By tracing just a central line on to the fabric you avoid the possibility of any drawn lines showing beyond the bias

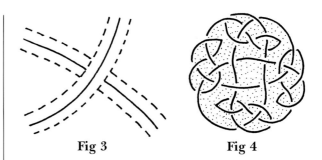

**Fig 3**          **Fig 4**

strapping when it is pinned in place.

**3** Cut around the outer drawn line of the Knot design so that the piece of fabric is the same circular shape as the design (Fig 4). Place the cut fabric on top of the traced design with all the drawn lines matching. Fold the fabric back along the centre dotted line and finger press it.

**4** Cut a square of fabric 13 x 13in (33 x 33cm) for the background. Fold in half vertically and press lightly. Use the fold as a guide for positioning the cut medallion fabric centrally on it – the folded line on the medallion fabric should be placed on the fold in the background fabric.

Pin the trimmed design on to the background in several places, then tack around the edge using 1/4in (6mm) long stitches and keeping them about 1/2in (1.2cm) from the edge of the design so that the appliqué is held firmly in place (Fig 5).

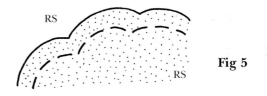

**Fig 5**

**5** If an extra fabric is to be used for the centre area, go back to the original traced design and from it trace just the centre shape onto paper, drawing a single line midway between the two parallel lines of the design as before (Fig 6). Cut this shape out and pin it onto the *right* side of the fabric chosen for the centre area, matching the grain arrow of the tracing with the straight grain of the fabric. Cut around the shape exactly – no extra seam allowance is needed.

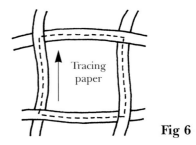

Tracing paper

**Fig 6**

Fig 2

**Fig 7**

Pin the piece in position in the centre of the design, matching the drawn lines on the tacked fabric with the cut edges of this extra piece. Tack in place (Fig 7).

***Cutting the Strips and Making Bias Tubes***
The strips for the Celtic Knot strapping must be cut on the bias of the fabric, i.e., diagonally across the weave. This is because bias-cut strips are very stretchy and can curve around the lines of the design without puckering. For this design 1in (2.5cm) wide bias strips are used. Although about 140in (355cm) of strips are needed for the design they can all be cut from a 14in (35.6cm) square of fabric, as they do not have to be in a continuous length.

**6** To cut the strips, place a single layer of fabric across one of the 45° lines on a cutting board, with the grain or weave of the fabric matching the grid on the cutting board. The fabric does not have to be trimmed to an exact 14in (35.6cm) square: an odd rectangular piece will do, as long as its area is at least as much as a 14in (35.6cm) square. Cut along the 45° line with a rotary cutter and ruler (Fig 8). Turn the fabric so that the cut edge is on the left and move the ruler over it until the cut edge lines up with the 1in (2.5cm) marking on the ruler. Cut along the right side of the ruler (Fig 9). Left-handers should cut their strips from the right, not the left. Repeat this across the fabric,

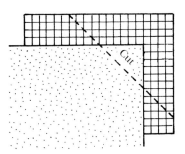

**Fig 8**

cutting 1in (2.5cm) wide strips each time, and also cutting more strips from the small triangle of fabric left after the initial diagonal cut.

**7** To process the bias strips into tubes a bias bar with a width of ¼in (6mm) is needed. With the right side of the fabric facing *outwards*, fold a 1in (2.5cm) wide bias strip of fabric in half lengthways. Using a smaller stitch than usual, machine a ¼in (6mm) seam down the length of the strip to make a tube. The stitched tube will *not* be pulled inside out – that is why the fabric is folded with the right side on the outside. Make a short sample length of tubing first and slide the bias bar into it. It needs to fit really snugly without any slack (Fig 10a). Once you are happy with the width of the tube, stitch all the bias strips in the same way. Trim the seams to a scant ⅛in (3mm) (Fig 10b). Slide the bar into a tube, twisting the fabric so that both seam and seam allowance lie across one flat side of the bar and cannot be seen from the other side (Fig 10c). Press firmly and continue to press as you slide the tube off the bar. A steam iron gives a good flat finish to the bias tubes. Press all the fabric tubes in this way. You do not need a continuous length of bias tubing for the design. The raw edges at the end of a tube are hidden under an overlying tube as it passes over it to make the woven design.

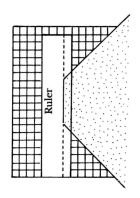

**Fig 9**

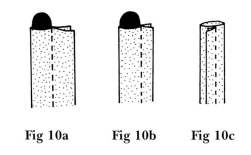

**Fig 10a**      **Fig 10b**      **Fig 10c**

**8** Take a length of pressed bias tubing and trim one end to neaten it. Starting anywhere in the central area of the design, pin the trimmed end of

## GILL SHARMAN

*'In my previous Sampler Quilt, I used so many colours that the effect was lost. This time I was determined to be disciplined and use what I liked best, ie. black, grey and a little red. I really enjoyed it.'*

pressed bias tubing at a junction of drawn lines where it will later be concealed beneath an overlying tube. The drawn guideline should lie midway beneath the tube. If an extra fabric has been tacked in place at the centre of the design, its raw edge should also lie midway under the bias tubing (Fig 11).

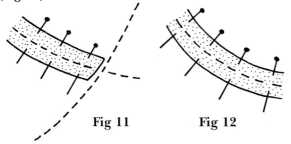

**Fig 11**       **Fig 12**

All the lines of this Celtic Knot design are curved, some more than others, so the bias tubing has to be carefully pinned and stitched to follow these curves. Pin and stitch the shorter inside edge of the tubing first. The longer outside edge can then be stretched slightly when sewing to fit the curve (Fig 12). If you fix the longer edge first, the shorter edge will finish up with little pleats in it. Finish each piece of tubing by trimming it so that it ends exactly at a junction where it will be hidden beneath an overlying tube. All starting and ending points are made at these underlying junctions (Fig 13).

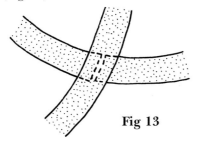

**Fig 13**

***Dealing with the 'Overs' and 'Unders'***
**9** The Celtic Knot design could be made with one continuous length of pressed tubing weaving over and under itself, but as long as each tube finishes hidden under an underlying tube, the effect is the same. Just pin and stitch each pressed tube as far as it lasts on the design, making sure it finishes

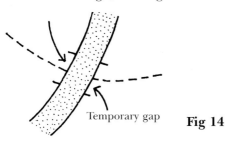

Temporary gap      **Fig 14**

hidden as in Fig 13. At a junction of lines where the tubing passes over another, a gap of 1/4–1/2in (6–12mm) must be left in the stitching so that the under tube can be pulled through at a later stage. Once this is in place the gap can then be stitched (Fig 14).

It is all too easy to forget to leave the gaps at each 'over' junction, so I mark them when pinning the tubing in place by pinning a spare length of tubing about 1in (2.5cm) long under the tube in the place to be left unstitched to remind me (Fig 15). Once the danger zone has been passed this piece can then be removed and used in the same way at the next 'over' junction. Do not pin the entire design, only as far as your piece of tubing will cover, finishing with the trimmed end at an 'under' junction.

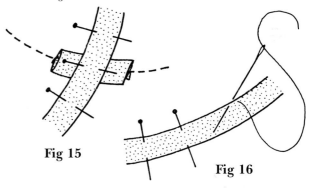

**Fig 15**       **Fig 16**

**10** Matching the thread to the tube fabric, not the background, sew both sides of the tube in turn to the background with small, even slip stitches, stitching the shorter inner edge first (Fig 16). When you reach a junction where the bias tubing needs to go *under* a section that has already been stitched in place, push the end of the tubing through the gap, using the points of a small pair of scissors to ease it under. Pull the tubing through and use the scissors to smooth the underneath layer flat. Stitch the gap in the top layer of tubing before continuing to pin and stitch the loose piece of tubing.

This design has four nasty turning points where the bias tubing has to be swung round sharply to make a point (Fig 17). To make the mitred corner,

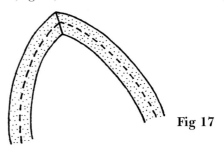

**Fig 17**

stitch along the pinned inner curve until about ¼in (6mm) from the corner. Position the tube at the far point where it will turn, about ⅛in (3mm) beyond the drawn corner, and catch the edge of the bias tubing with a large pin pushed down into the background fabric (Fig 18). Angle the pin towards you and bring it up through the fabric as shown in Fig 19.

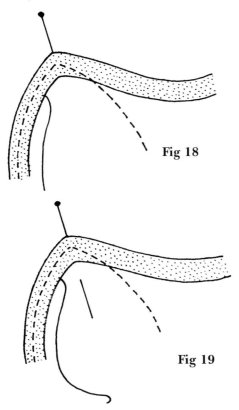

**Fig 18**

**Fig 19**

Now pull the tubing sharply into position over the drawn guideline. Use a small pair of scissors to tuck the extra fabric behind the main tubing to form a mitre while holding the tubing firmly in position (Fig 20). When the mitre looks good hold it in position with your thumb. Withdraw the pin

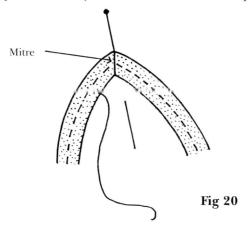

Mitre

**Fig 20**

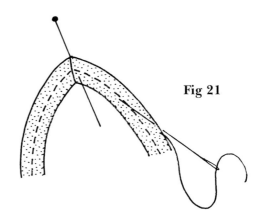

**Fig 21**

slightly and re-pin its point through the mitre to fix it while you sew (Fig 21). Do not stitch the mitre itself, just the edges of the tubing as usual. Continue to pin and stitch the design.

**11**  Once all the pressed tubing has been stitched into place, the design is complete and the tacking can be removed. The thickness of the block can be reduced by cutting away the background fabric from behind the Celtic Knot. Cut away behind the open areas of the design between the bias tubing. Do not attempt to cut away behind the tubing itself as it is just too narrow to do safely. If you feel too nervous to try any of this, don't worry, as it is not compulsory. However, it does make the whole piece easier to quilt, so the choice is yours. To cut the backing away, turn the block to the back and with your fingers pull the background away from the appliqué and make a small cut in the background fabric. Now carefully cut away the backing up to ¼in (6mm) from the stitching lines. Do this in all the open areas of the design.

**12**  Trim the finished block to an exact 13in (33cm) square, or to whatever size you feel suits your design. Add the inner framing strips and trim the block to exactly 14in (35.6cm) square, then add the sashing strips. See page 130 for adding framing strips and sashing.

## MACHINE PIECING

# DELECTABLE MOUNTAINS

This lovely design is combined with large squares to make the block for the New Sampler Quilt (Fig 1, page 42). It also makes a striking border for a quilt. I first saw this clever, quick method of making the design in a magazine where it had been devised by Sheila Scawen, a very experienced and talented quilter and teacher. It combines strip patchwork with the quick machined triangles shown in the block on page 29. The Delectable Mountain arrangement of strips does

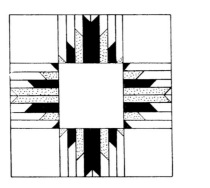

**Fig 1**

not make a square but a rectangle. The maths involved in devising different sizes for the block is surprisingly tricky because of all the seam allowances to be taken into consideration, so at the end of the instructions for the block I have given some alternative sizings and measurements for future reference for borders.

## COLOUR CHOICES

The saw-toothed edged Delectable Mountains can be made from one fabric plus a background, or from two fabrics combined (Figs 2a and 2b). I used two fabrics for the Delectable Mountains and took one of them for the centre square. You may find it helpful to make the four Mountain pieces before deciding on what looks best in the centre and the four corners of the block. The large centre square looks less empty if a patterned fabric is used, or if it is broken up with a quilting design later.

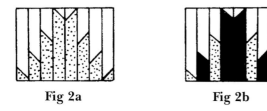

**Fig 2a**          **Fig 2b**

## CONSTRUCTION

*For the design in Fig 2a:* If *one* fabric plus a background fabric are to be used for the design, cut four squares of each of the two fabrics, each measuring $4^7/8$ x $4^7/8$in (12.4 x 12.4cm).

*For the design in Fig 2b:* If *two* fabrics plus a background fabric are to be used for the design, cut four squares of the background fabric and two squares of each of the two Delectable Mountain fabrics, each measuring $4^7/8$ x $4^7/8$in (12.4 x 12.4cm).

**1** Arrange the squares in pairs, one background fabric paired with a Mountain fabric. Place the pairs right sides together *exactly* on top of each other.

Draw a diagonal line on the top fabric as Fig 3.
**2** Pin the squares together and machine a line of small stitches on *either side* of the drawn line exactly $1/4$in (6mm) away from the line (Fig 4). This technique was also used to construct the quick machined triangles in the block on page 31.

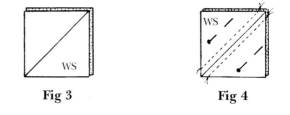

**Fig 3**          **Fig 4**

**3** Once all four pairs have been stitched, place on the cutting board and using a rotary cutter and ruler cut along the drawn lines so that the squares fall into two halves. Open each half out: each should now form a square divided diagonally into two fabrics (Fig 5). Press each of the eight squares from the front,

**Fig 5**

four with the seam allowances pressed towards the Mountain fabric and the other four towards the background fabric.

If you've used *two* fabrics for the Mountains, separate the squares into matching pairs of the same combination of fabrics and then press the seams of each pair from the front, with one pressed towards the Mountain fabric and the other towards the background fabric.
**4** Measure each pressed square carefully – it's important they all now measure the same $4^1/2$ x $4^1/2$in (11.4 x 11.4cm). If a square is too small, press with a steam iron and stretch the square out to get it to the right measurement. If this is not successful, fold the square back into a triangle and re-stitch the seam until the correct sizing is achieved. Squares that are too large can be trimmed down to size, making sure that the diagonal seam still runs from corner to corner of the square.
**5** Group the pressed squares in matching pairs (each pair should be made up of the same two fabrics) and place them right sides together, matching the seams and the fabrics. Hopefully the seams of one of the squares will be pressed in the opposite direction to the seams of the other square (Fig 6).

Place the squares on a cutting board, arranging each pair as in Fig 6 with the seams running diagonally from top right corner to bottom left and the Mountain fabric in the bottom right-hand half of each square. Check that each pair of squares is lying exactly one on top of the other. Do not pin them as the pins get in the way of the rotary cutter.

**6** Using a rotary cutter and ruler, cut one pair of matched squares into four equal vertical strips, cutting through both layers at once. Each strip should measure 1$^1$/8in (2.8cm) in width (Fig 7).

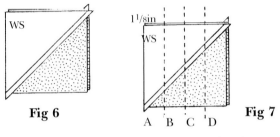

**Fig 6**　　　　　　　　**Fig 7**

**7** Pick up the two layered strips marked D in Fig 7, open them out and place them right side *up* together in the arrangement shown in Fig 8. Pick up the pair of strips marked C in Fig 7. Place the top strip right side *up* to the *left* of strips D. Place the other strip right side *up* to the *right* of strips D (Fig 9). Place strips B and then strips A on either side of strips D and C in the same way, following the arrangement in Fig 10.

**Fig 8**

D　D

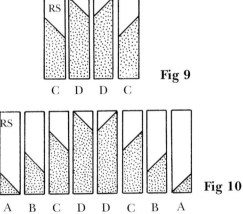

C　D　D　C

**Fig 9**

A　B　C　D　D　C　B　A

**Fig 10**

If you've used *two* fabrics for the Mountains, repeat the cutting process with a set of squares that use the second Mountain fabric. Arrange these strips in the same arrangement as Fig 10 alongside the first set. Exchange the C strips from the first set with the C strips in the second set. Repeat this with the A strips (Fig 11). Stitch together these sets of eight strips before going on to cut the remaining pairs of squares, unless you have a lot of space and a very organised mind.

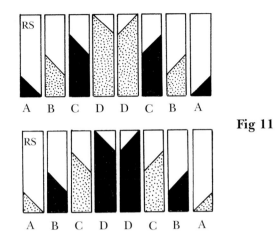

A　B　C　D　D　C　B　A

**Fig 11**

A　B　C　D　D　C　B　A

If you've used just *one* fabric for the Mountains, cut and stitch the strips one set at a time for the same reason: if you get the sets mixed up it can take a lot of time and nervous energy to sort them all out again.

**8** Stitch together the eight strips, making sure the top and bottom edges match exactly as in Fig 12. Press the centre seam open, as this helps the balanced look of the design. Press the remaining seams away from the centre as in Fig 12.

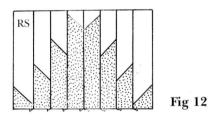

**Fig 12**

**9** Measure the four stitched sets of strips. They should measure 4$^1$/2 x 5$^1$/2in (11.4 x 14cm). Don't worry if your measurements do not match these, as long as they are *no larger* than this or the finished block will be too big for the quilt.

What is important is that all of the rectangles measure the same as each other. Check the seams and adjust any that are obviously inaccurate. Use a steam iron to help get all four rectangles to the same size. Try to resist the temptation to trim bits off the strips as this can spoil the balanced look of the block.

**10** Arrange your fabrics with the completed rectangles of Mountains to finalise your choice for the centre square and corners. If the rectangles measure 4$^1$/2 x 5$^1$/2in (11.4 x 14cm) cut a square for the centre measuring 5$^1$/2 x 5$^1$/2in (14 x 14cm) and four squares for the corners measuring 4$^1$/2 x 4$^1$/2in (11.4 x 11.4cm). If your rectangles do not have these measurements, don't worry – if the centre and corner squares are cut to match *your*

rectangles, the block will fit together nicely. Cut the centre square to match the longer side and the corner squares to match the shorter side of your rectangles (Fig 13).

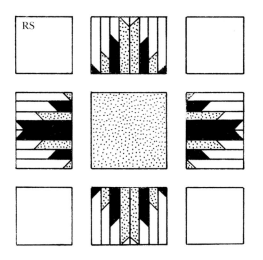

**Fig 13**

**11** Pin and stitch the shapes together in rows (Fig 14). From the front, press the seams towards the squares, away from the pieced rectangles.
**12** Stitch the rows together to make the block, matching seams carefully. Press the seams towards the centre of the block, ironing from the front.
**13** The block should now measure 13½ x 13½in (34.3 x 34.3cm). An inner border of strips cut 1¼in (3.2cm) wide can be added and the block then trimmed down exactly to a 14in (35.6cm) square. Finally, add the sashing strips. See page 130 for adding framing strips and sashing.

---

### GWEN BRYSON

*'Having moved from Suffolk to Gloucestershire, I worked Lynne's New Sampler Quilt by correspondence course. Each month I waited eagerly for the postman to bring me the notes for the next two blocks. The instructions were precise and easy to follow and I felt as if Lynne was at my elbow talking me through each design!'*

---

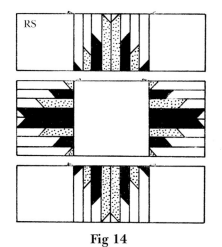

**Fig 14**

### SOME ALTERNATIVE SIZES FOR THE DELECTABLE MOUNTAINS

*A larger rectangle measuring a final size of 11 x 7in (27.9 x 17.4cm):*
This can be used together with another Mountains rectangle to make a block which, with borders added as in Fig 15, will finish up as a cushion-sized design. The initial squares are cut 8⅜ x 8⅜in (21.3 x 21.3cm). Once stitched and cut into the pieced squares they need to measure 8 x 8in (20.3 x 20.3cm). Cut the squares into four vertical strips as before, each measuring exactly 2in (5cm) wide.

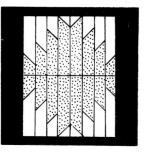

**Fig 15**

*A smaller rectangle measuring a final size of 5½ x 8in (14 x 20.3cm):*
This is suitable for borders on a quilt (Fig 16). Cut initial squares 6⅜ x 6⅜in (16.2 x 16.2cm). They should measure 6 x 6in (15.2 x 15.2cm) after stitching and cutting into pieced squares. Cut the squares into vertical strips as before, each strip measuring exactly 1½in (3.8cm) in width.

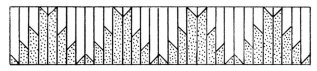

**Fig 16**

## HAND PIECING WITH APPLIQUÉ

# CAROLINA LILY

This is a traditional block that combines pieced patchwork with appliqué, as do so many of the American quilt designs. Although it is a square design it is usually seen in a quilt with the square on point, that is, turned through 45° so that it makes a diamond shape with the corners at the top, bottom and sides. To achieve this effect I have drafted a smaller version of the block than usual, turned it through 45° and added corners so that the final block is square with the Carolina Lily

within it on point (Fig 1). This is not an easy block to draft, as it combines long diamonds with triangles and squares. If you wanted a larger version of the block given here, it would be easier to look for it in a book of block patterns than to spend ages calculating all those tricky measurements. There are many variations of the Lily block, some of which have been simplified slightly to make piecing easier. This version combines piecing, stems from Celtic bias strips and appliquéd leaves.

**Fig 1**

### COLOUR CHOICES

The lily is made from two fabrics combined in the petals and a third forming each flower base and stem. Any of these three fabrics can be used to make the appliqué leaves. The lilies are set in a background fabric which can also be used as the extra large corners of the block, or another fabric could be chosen for this. I suggest you leave the decision about the corner fabric until the rest of the block is complete, then you can place the block on the fabrics and see which one looks best.

### CONSTRUCTION

**1** Make card templates by tracing the seven shapes from Fig 2 (page 48), cutting them out and sticking them on the card, or by using template plastic. Mark the directional arrows, as these show how the templates should be positioned on the grain or weave of the fabric. Also mark the midpoint O on template B. Trim the drawn lines away as you cut each template out to prevent the shapes becoming larger than the originals.

**2** On the wrong side of each fabric draw accurately around the templates using a sharp marking pencil and matching the direction of the arrows with the grain of the fabric. The drawn lines mark the stitching lines. Allow at least 1/2in (1.2cm) between each drawn outline so that the seam allowance of 1/4in (6mm) can be added to each shape when cutting out.

To make the four diamonds of the lily flower lie

comfortably together, the grain or weave of the fabric needs special consideration. The diamonds should be arranged as shown in Fig 3a, so half the pieces must be cut as a mirror image. Draw round the diamond template (Fig 2 A), matching the grain arrow with the weave of the fabric. Then *reverse* the template on the fabric and draw round it to make a mirror image (Fig 3b). For the lily flowers you will need three of shape A and three of shape A reversed from *each* of the two lily fabrics.

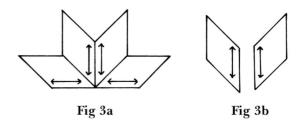

**Fig 3a**          **Fig 3b**

From the third fabric, three of shape B is needed (this fabric will also be used later for the bias stems). Mark the midpoint O in the seam allowance of the B shapes.

From the background fabric you need three of shape C, six of shape D, two of shape E, one of shape F and one of shape G.

**3** Cut out each shape to include the 1/4in (6mm) seam allowance, either by eye or by using a rotary cutter and ruler. The width of the seam allowance is not critical but is very helpful if cut accurately, as then the edges of the fabrics line up as you match the drawn stitching lines.

Templates F and G show the position of the bias stems which are appliquéd to the block. The real outline is shown as parallel dotted lines with a stronger line between them. Trace just this middle line on to the *front* of fabric shapes F and G. Use a light box if necessary or dressmaker's carbon paper. The single line will act as a positioning guide for the stems when they are laid onto the block at a later stage.

**4** Fig 4 (page 49) shows the arrangement of pieces to make the block. Follow this carefully and arrange the cut fabric pieces on a flat surface or pin in position on a polystyrene tile or board. Final decisions can be made on the effectiveness of the fabric choices at this stage.

**5** Begin by piecing together each lily flower. Arrange the four long diamonds as shown in Fig 3a, taking care to position them so that the centre seam is on the straight grain of the fabric. Place two of the diamonds together with right sides facing along the two sides to be joined. Pin and

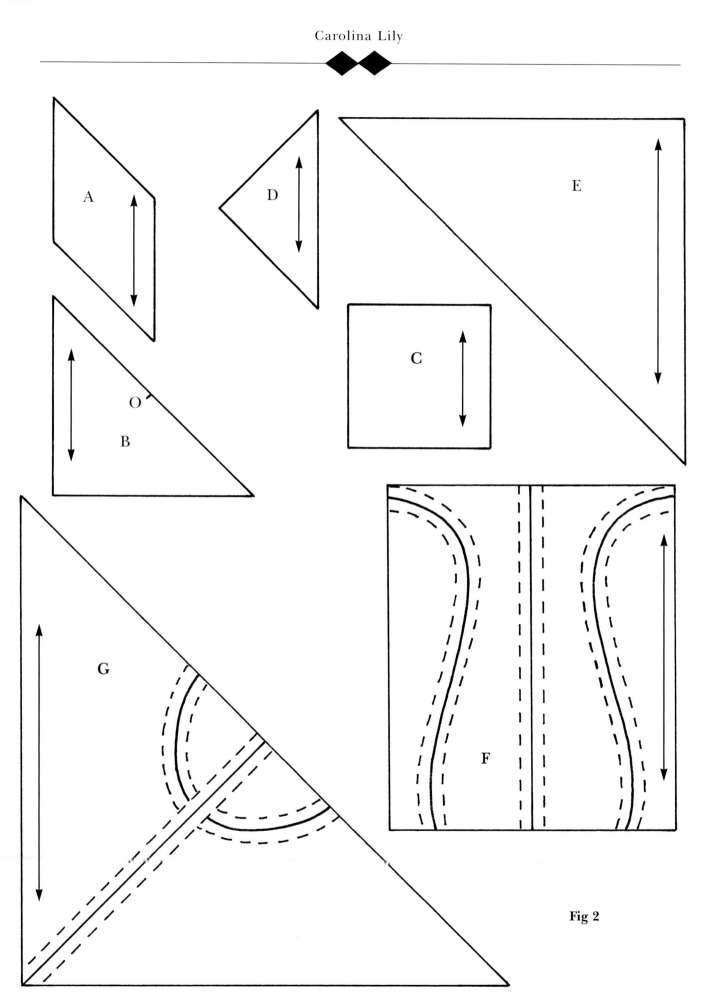

A

D

E

C

O

B

G

F

**Fig 2**

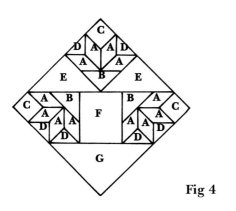

**Fig 4**

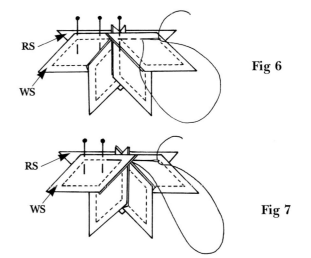

**Fig 6**

**Fig 7**

stitch along the marked lines, following the method used for piecing the Tangled Star block on page 26 (known as American Piecing). Stitch from corner to corner of the drawn design without stitching into the seam allowances. Open the two diamonds out and pin the third diamond to the second, matching the drawn seam lines. Stitch this seam. Pin and stitch the fourth diamond to the lily in the same way. Do not press any seams until the whole block is complete, as there is no set rule for which way each seam is to be pressed. Once it is finished the seams can be pressed whichever way avoids too much bulk at the back of the work.

**6** With right sides facing, pin piece B to the joined diamonds, matching the corners and drawn lines as in Fig 5. Position the centre of the four diamonds at the midpoint mark on piece B.

**7** Now add to each lily flower one square (C) and two triangles (D). Follow the arrangement in Fig 8a for the centre lily and the arrangements in Figs 8b and 8c for the other two lilies. All three lilies have a different positioning of pieces C and D – follow Figs 8a, 8b and 8c to get this right.

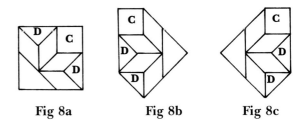

**Fig 8a**      **Fig 8b**      **Fig 8c**

To join shapes C and D to the main lily flower means stitching them into an angle, called setting-in, which is easier by hand than by machine. Beginning with square C, match the corners of the drawn lines of the seam to be stitched with pins in the usual way, working from the outer edge towards the inner corner. Add more pins along the seamline, matching the marked lines (Fig 9). Stitch to the inner corner of the design and make a backstitch (Fig 10). Swing the square round to line up with the edge of the second side of the lily. Match the drawn lines and pin. Push the centre seam allowances to one side, clear of the seam, and stitch along the drawn line as usual

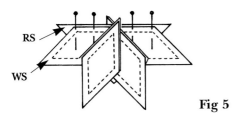

**Fig 5**

Pin close to the centre cluster of seams but not at the centre junction itself. Begin stitching with the diamond shapes uppermost until approaching the centre junction. Push the seam allowances away from the stitching area and match the marked corner of the stitched diamond to the midpoint on piece B by pushing a pin through both points until the head is on the surface of the diamond fabric. Reposition the pin at right angles to the seam (Fig 6). Stitch up to the seam and make a backstitch. Pass the needle through the corner of the stitched diamond into the corner of the last diamond, bypassing the two middle diamonds (Fig 7). Backstitch to pull all the seams together tightly and continue sewing. Repeat this process with the other two lily flowers.

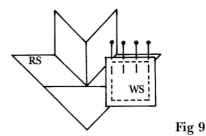

**Fig 9**

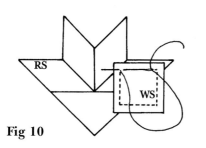

**Fig 10**

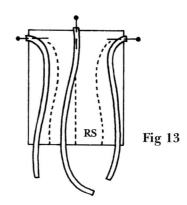

**Fig 13**

(Fig 11). Join the two D triangles to the lily in the same way. Complete each lily unit as in Figs 8a, 8b and 8c.

**8** The curving stems of this block are made from bias tubes constructed in exactly the same way as in the Celtic Knot block. Three lengths of pressed tube are needed, one 8in (20.3cm) for the centre stem and two 7in (17.8cm) for the side stems. Make and press these, following the instructions for the Celtic Knot block on page 37.

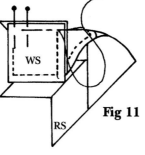

**Fig 11**

**9** The Carolina Lily block is assembled in three sections (Fig 12). Join the two triangles E to the lily shown in Fig 8a. This completes the top section.

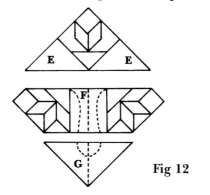

**Fig 12**

Pin the trimmed ends of the three Celtic tubes on to the *right* side of piece F, over the drawn lines of the stems (Fig 13). The loose ends of the tubes will be stitched on to piece F later once the block is joined together. Pin and stitch the two lilies to the long sides of piece F as in Fig 12, at the same time stitching through the stems where they are pinned on to piece F. You will probably have to stitch with stab stitches at this point because of the thickness of the pinned layers.

Join the top section to the middle section, matching seams carefully and stitching through the pinned stem in the centre.

Stitch piece G to the centre section of the block to complete it, matching the drawn stem guidelines.

**10** Press the block from the front, letting the seams lie in whichever direction avoids too much bulk at the back. They are never pressed open as the hand-sewn stitches are not strong enough.

**11** Pin the side stems in position, pinning the inside curves first as described in the instructions for the Celtic Knot block on page 39. Trim each end so that it butts against the centre seamline (Fig 14). Stitch the side stems to the block, using the method detailed for the Celtic Knot block.

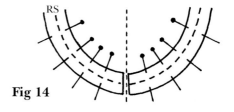

**Fig 14**

Because it is better to stitch the shorter side of a curve first, start stitching from the bottom to the point where the curve begins to swing the other way, roughly halfway along (Fig 15). Remove the needle, leaving the length of thread hanging loose, and restart from the other end of the stem, stitching the shorter side of the curve first. Continue to stitch this entire side of the stem. Finish off the stitching at the back as usual. Re-thread the needle with the long loose end of thread and complete the stitching on the remaining side of the stem (Fig 16). The centre stem is

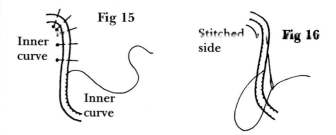

**Fig 15**

Inner curve

Inner curve

Stitched side

**Fig 16**

JEAN HATHERLY

'My quilt is fully hand-quilted because I get great satisfaction and enjoyment from this. It has been with me for two years and my constant companion for the last six months. My husband has named it "Grounds for Divorce".'

then pinned over the drawn line on piece F and stitched in position. It will cover the two raw edges of the side stems. Trim the bottom edge in a V shape to match the edges of the block.

**12** Trace the leaf shape given in Fig 17 twice on to the smooth side of freezer paper. Cut out the shapes and iron them shiny side down onto the *wrong* side of the chosen fabric. Cut out with a 1/4in (6mm) seam allowance. Clip the curve nearly but not quite to the freezer paper. Do not clip near the pointed end of the leaf shape (Fig 18a). Carefully peel off the paper, replacing it in exactly the same position but with the shiny side *upwards* and pin the freezer paper on to the fabric (Fig 18b). I use one or two small pins to stop the paper moving.

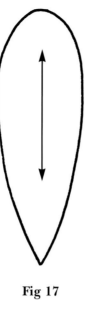

**Fig 17**

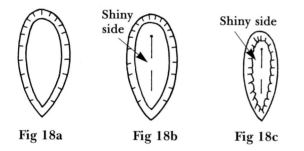

**Fig 18a**    **Fig 18b**    **Fig 18c**

Use as firm an ironing surface as possible: a thick piece of cardboard with a piece of spare fabric on it to protect the surface is a good emergency board if your usual ironing surface is not firm enough. Set the iron to a wool setting and do not use steam. Using the side of the iron rather than the point, nudge the seam allowance of fabric over onto the freezer paper, easing in the fullness on the curves a little at a time until all the seam allowance is stuck down on the paper (Fig 18c). Take care not to press in any tiny pleats on the outer edge but keep the curve smooth. If there are any areas you are not happy with, peel the fabric back and re-press in the correct position. If the folded fabric at the pointed section of the leaf does not tuck flat and shows from the front of the appliqué, either tuck it under while stitching the appliqué on to the background, or secure it with a dab of glue from a glue-stick. Provided the glue is water-soluble it will not harm the fabric. Arrange the two leaves on the block and pin or tack them

in place. Sew each one on to the background with small slip stitches, using thread to match the appliqué, not the background. Once the appliqué has been completed, cut the backing fabric away to 1/4in (6mm) from the stitching line so the freezer paper can be removed.

**Fig 19**

**13** Press the block. From the fabric to be used for the final large corners surrounding the block (Fig 1) cut two squares each 7½in (19cm) square. Cut each square in half diagonally (Fig 19).

Pin and stitch the long side of one triangle to one side of the block, right sides facing. It should be slightly longer than the square, so balance the extra length equally at either end (Fig 20). Stitch right across the fabric from edge to edge, not just from the corners of the drawn shapes. Press the triangle with seams outwards from the block.

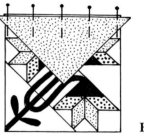

**Fig 20**

In the same way, pin and stitch a triangle to the opposite side of the block. Press the triangle outwards. Pin and stitch the remaining two triangles to the sides of the block and press outwards.

**14** Place the completed block on to a cutting board and trim down the sides to 1/4in (6mm) beyond the four corners of the Carolina Lily block (Fig 21). The block should now measure about 13in (13cm) square. Cut and add 1¼in (3.2cm) wide framing strips. Once these are stitched in place trim the block down to 14in (35.6cm) square. Finally, add the sashing strips. See page 130 for adding framing strips and sashing.

**Fig 21**

## MACHINE PIECING

# QUICK BOW TIE

**B**ow Tie is a traditional patchwork block (Fig 1 page 54), usually constructed with two templates in the American patchwork tradition, as used in the Tangled Star block. This quick and clever method is based on squares of fabric which are folded and machine-stitched to give the Bow Tie effect. Once you have got the hang of it the blocks can be chain-stitched and mass-produced with amazing speed.

Several students have produced wonderful bed

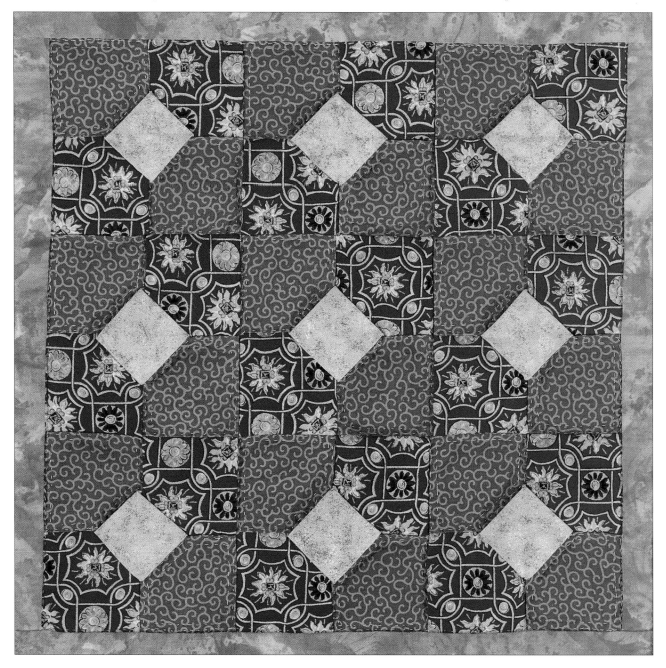

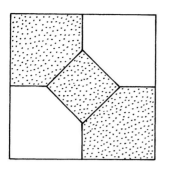

**Fig 1**

quilts using a Bow Tie block based on 3in (7.6cm) squares of fabric which finishes up as a 5in (12.7cm) block. This size would be too big to use for the Sampler Quilt, so I have offered two designs as alternative choices for the block. One uses cut fabric squares measuring 2½in (6.3cm) to make the design of nine Bow Ties shown in Fig 2a and in the photograph on page 53. The other uses 2in (5cm) cut squares of fabric to make a block of 16 Bow Ties as in Fig 2b. This second block is much more fiddly than the first. I suggest that you make just one Bow Tie unit from both designs to try out the technique. If you enjoy working on a small scale, make the second design; but if it proves too fiddly for you, choose the larger nine-patch design. Either looks good as the finished block in the quilt.

## COLOUR CHOICES

In the nine-patch design (Fig 2a) each Bow Tie is placed diagonally on a background fabric. It is more interesting if the Bow Ties vary in colour and Fig 3a shows an arrangement of Bow Ties in two

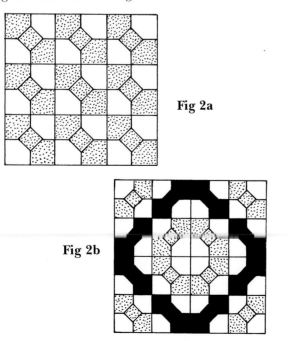

**Fig 2a**

**Fig 2b**

colours on a background. Fig 3b shows a design of Bow Ties in one fabric with each knot in a second fabric. More fabrics could be used for the Bow Ties if you prefer that effect, of course. For the more complex design in Fig 2b I used two fabrics for the Bow Ties with one background fabric.

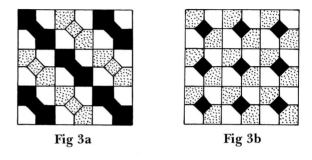

**Fig 3a**          **Fig 3b**

## CONSTRUCTION
### *The Nine Bow Tie Design*

Make up nine Bow Tie units in the method described below, using whichever fabrics suit your plan.

*For the design in Fig 3a:* Cut fifteen squares in one Bow Tie fabric and twelve squares in another Bow Tie fabric, all measuring 2½ x 2½in (6.3 x 6.3cm). For the background cut eighteen squares each 2½ x 2½in (6.3 x 6.3cm). Assemble five Bow Tie units in one fabric plus background and four Bow Tie units in the second fabric plus background (Fig 4).

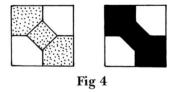

**Fig 4**

*For the design in Fig 3b:* Cut eighteen squares for the Bow Ties in one fabric and nine squares for the knots in a second fabric, each measuring 2½ x 2½in (6.3 x 6.3cm). For the background cut eighteen squares 2½ x 2½in (6.3 x 6.3cm).

**1** Cut three squares of fabric for the Bow Tie itself, each measuring 2½ x 2½in (6.3 x 6.3cm). Cut two squares of fabric for the background, each measuring 2½ x 2½in (6.3 x 6.3cm) (see Fig 5).

Bow tie                    Background

**Fig 5**

**2** Fold one of the Bow Tie squares in a half with right side *out*. This forms the knot of the Bow Tie (Fig 6).

Place a square of Bow Tie fabric on a flat surface right side *up*. Place the folded knot strip on top of it with the fold running down the centre from top to bottom and the raw edges to the left (Fig 7).

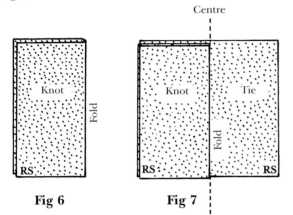

**Fig 6**　　　**Fig 7**

**3** Now place a square of background fabric on the top, right side *down*, matching the raw edges of the new square with the raw edges of the underneath layers. You should have a sandwich of the two different fabric squares with their right sides facing and the folded knot rectangle between them (Fig 8).

**4** Pin the top edges together (Fig 9). Machine a seam ¼in (6mm) from the top edges through all the layers (Fig 10).

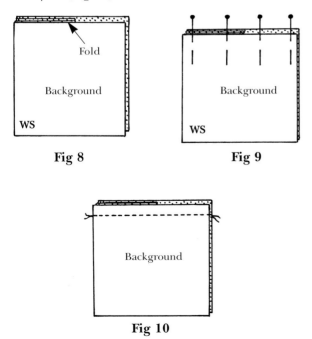

**Fig 8**　　　**Fig 9**

**Fig 10**

**5** Fold both squares of fabric back from the knot (Fig 11).

**6** Repeat this sequence: Place a square of Bow Tie fabric on a flat surface with right side *up*. Place the folded knot strip on it, again with the fold running down the centre from top to bottom and the raw edges to the left (Fig 12).

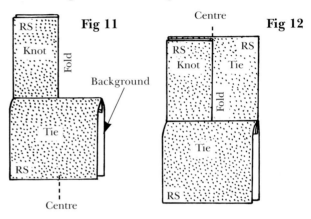

**Fig 11**　　　**Fig 12**

**7** Now place the last square of background fabric on the top, right side down, carefully matching the top raw edge with the top raw edges of the other fabrics as before (Fig 13).

**8** Pin along the top edges through all the layers (Fig 14). Stitch a seam ¼in (6mm) from these top edges (Fig 15).

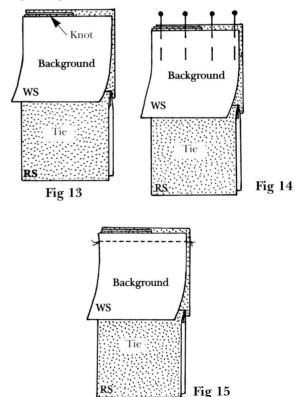

**Fig 13**　　　**Fig 14**

**Fig 15**

PAT MITCHELL

*'My colours were inspired by an exciting production of Henry V at Shakespeares's
Globe Theatre. I keep thinking of all those banners flying at Agincourt!'*

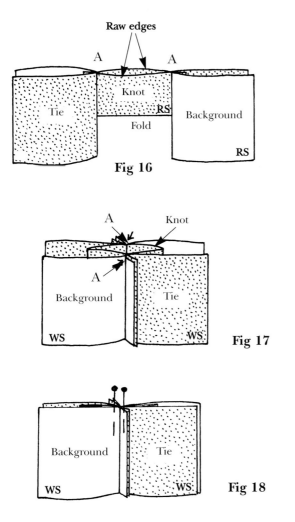

Fig 16

Fig 17

Fig 18

**9** Pull the fabric squares back from the knot. It should look rather strange, hopefully as in Fig 16.
**10** Now comes the cunning bit. Separate the two raw edges of the knot strip. Pull them apart and match the two opposite seams, each marked in Fig 16 and 17 as A. Finger press the seams at A in opposite directions (Fig 17). Pin the two seams together, matching them carefully (Fig 18).
**11** Match the top edges of the squares and of the knot that is sandwiched between them, taking care not to catch in any odd folds of fabric. Pin these edges together (Fig 19). Stitch through the layers with a 1/4in (6mm) seam (Fig 20).
**12** Open out the block to reveal the completed

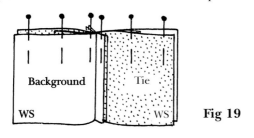

Fig 19

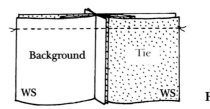

Fig 20

Bow Tie with its knot. If there are any little pleats or untidy corners in the knot, check the long stitched edge. There is probably one edge of fabric in all those layers that has dropped lower than the others. Unpick just that section, re-pin and stitch again. Press the Bow Tie from the front.
**13** Assemble the nine Bow Tie units using the same combination for both the design in Fig 3a and 3b: two squares for the Tie, one square for the knot and two squares of the background fabric (Fig 21) Press each completed unit and arrange them in the chosen design. Pin and stitch the units into three rows, matching seams carefully. Finally join the rows to make the block.

Fig 21

### The Sixteen Bow Tie Design
Make up sixteen smaller Bow Tie units in the method described for the units in the Nine Bow Tie design, using whichever fabrics suit your plan.

*For the design in Fig 2b:* Cut twenty-four squares of one Bow Tie fabric and twenty-four squares of a second Bow Tie fabric, each 2 x 2in (5 x 5cm). For the background cut thirty-two squares of the chosen fabric, each 2 x 2in (5 x 5cm). Make eight Bow Tie units, using one Bow Tie fabric plus the background and eight Bow Tie units using the second fabric plus the background. The method for making the smaller 2in (5cm) squares is just as straightforward as making the larger squares until the pinning and stitching of that final long seam (Fig 20). I find it best to begin in the centre and work out in the opposite direction for the other half. Press the sixteen completed units and arrange them in the design shown in Fig 2b. Pin and stitch the units into four rows, matching seams carefully. Finally join the rows to complete the block.

The finished block, whether you have chosen the Nine or Sixteen Bow Tie design, should measure about 12½ x 12½in (31.7 x 31.7cm). Add the inner framing strips and trim the block to an exact 14in (35.6cm) square. Finally add the sashing strips (see page 130).

## HAND STITCHED FREEZER PAPER APPLIQUÉ

# CLAMSHELL

The Clamshell design is frequently found in antique quilts as pieced shapes or providing a rich overall quilting design. It is usually one of those patterns that people love but avoid because of the high-risk nervous breakdown factor!

Template kits for English patchwork have been around for many years, although the problems involved with the joining of the shapes have given it limited popularity.

I have always treated the shape as an appliqué,

laying down the clamshells in rows on a background fabric and overlapping them row by row (Fig 2). Regular horizontal lines are drawn on the background square to help keep the clamshells level. The limitation of the technique is that each row overlaps the row above, so the bottom row has to completely cover the background fabric with its points hanging off the bottom. These are trimmed off after the final row is stitched in place.

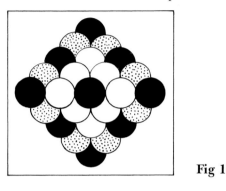

**Fig 1**

For the design in this New Sampler Quilt block (Fig 1) I have cheated in that the overlapped rows of clamshells are worked from the top downwards and also from the bottom upwards. The area of raw edges in the centre where both rows meet is covered by a row of whole circles appliquéd across both halves of the design. The only way to make sure that everything finishes up in the right place is to draw the design very lightly on the background fabric as a guide to positioning, as with an appliqué design.

**Fig 2**

## COLOUR CHOICES

Several colours or shades can be used for the clamshells which can be arranged in a variety of patterns on a background fabric (see Figs 3a, 3b, 3c). If you are unsure, try photocopying the design and colouring it in or, better still, make some clamshells in each fabric and then arrange them on the background fabric to see which pattern is the most pleasing. The design is not large, so the background fabric is reduced to a smaller square with a wider inner frame added.

**Fig 3a**

**Fig 3b**

**Fig 3c**

## CONSTRUCTION

**1** The template for the clamshell is based on a circle with a 2in (5cm) diameter. The bottom edge (marked with a dotted line in Fig 4a) has had a ¼in (6mm) seam added to make working with the fine point of the clamshells easier. The second template (Fig 4b on page 60) is for the five complete circles that make the middle row of the design.

The technique for this block uses freezer paper as a base for the clamshells and circles. Make the two templates by tracing the shapes from Figs 4a and 4b, cutting them out and sticking them on to card or by using template plastic. Draw round the clamshell template on the non-shiny side of freezer paper using a really sharp pencil to keep the shape accurate. If freezer paper is not available, the outer wrapping from packs of photocopy

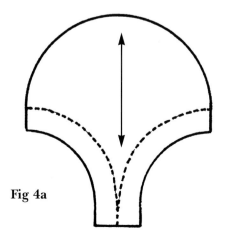

**Fig 4a**

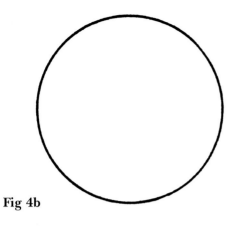

**Fig 4b**

paper is an excellent substitute. Cut out twenty clamshells from the freezer paper.

Draw round the circle template in the same way to make five freezer paper circles and cut these out.

**2** Iron the twenty freezer paper clamshells shiny side *down* on the *back* of the chosen fabrics leaving about ¹/₂in (1.2cm) between each clamshell to allow for seam allowances. Match the drawn arrow on the template with the grain of the fabric (Fig 5).

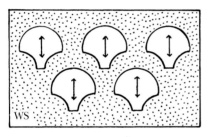

**Fig 5**

**3** Cut out each clamshell adding a ¹/₄in (6mm) seam allowance to the top curved edge *only* (Fig 6). The bottom two edges already have the seam allowances added to them. The ¹/₄in (6mm) seam allowance around the top edge does not have to be carefully measured but can be cut by eye.

**4** Peel the freezer paper off the fabric and replace it shiny side *up* on the *wrong* side of the fabric clamshell in exactly the same position, matching the bottom edges of both fabric and paper. Pin the freezer paper on to the fabric (Fig 7). I use two pins to stop the paper moving.

Using the side of an iron, nudge the seam allowance of fabric over on to the freezer paper,

easing in the fullness a little at a time so that it sticks to the paper. Don't worry too much if the iron touches the surface of the freezer paper. Take care not to press any tiny pleats in the outer edge but keep the curve smooth (Fig 8). If there are any areas you are not happy with, just peel the fabric back and re-press in the correct position.

**5** Iron the five paper circles shiny side *down* on the *back* of the chosen fabrics, leaving about ¹/₂in (1.2cm) between each circle to allow for seam allowances. Cut around each circle adding a ¹/₄in (6mm) seam allowance. Peel off the paper and reposition it in exactly the same position but with the shiny side facing *upwards*. Do not clip the seam allowance, but press it over the freezer paper in the same way as the clamshells (Fig 9).

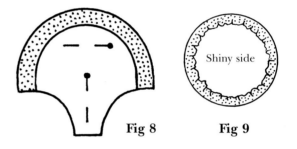

**Fig 8**          **Fig 9**

**6** Cut a square of background fabric 12 x 12in (30.5 x 30.5cm). Fold it into quarters and press lightly. Trace the design layout from Fig 10 onto paper, including the dotted centre markings.

Place the unfolded fabric square over the drawn design, positioning the fold lines over the dotted lines on the design and matching the centres. This is half the finished design. Draw very lightly with a marking pencil just inside the lines of the design to give an indication of where the clamshells and circles will be positioned. Do not draw exact outlines in case these show around the edges of the appliquéd shapes after stitching. Once the lines are marked on the fabric, turn the background square through 180°, realign the centres and the line of circles and trace the remaining opposite section of the design (as in Fig 1). If the fabric is not fine enough to trace through, use a light box.

**7** Arrange the prepared shapes on the background, checking that the design works well. Now is the time to make any changes if needed. The clamshells are arranged and stitched in rows, so the first row is just one clamshell (Fig 11 page 63).

**8** Position the first clamshell on the background fabric and press. This will fix it on the background while you stitch it in place, although you may also want to pin it if you feel it is insecure. Using

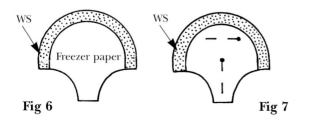

**Fig 6**                    **Fig 7**

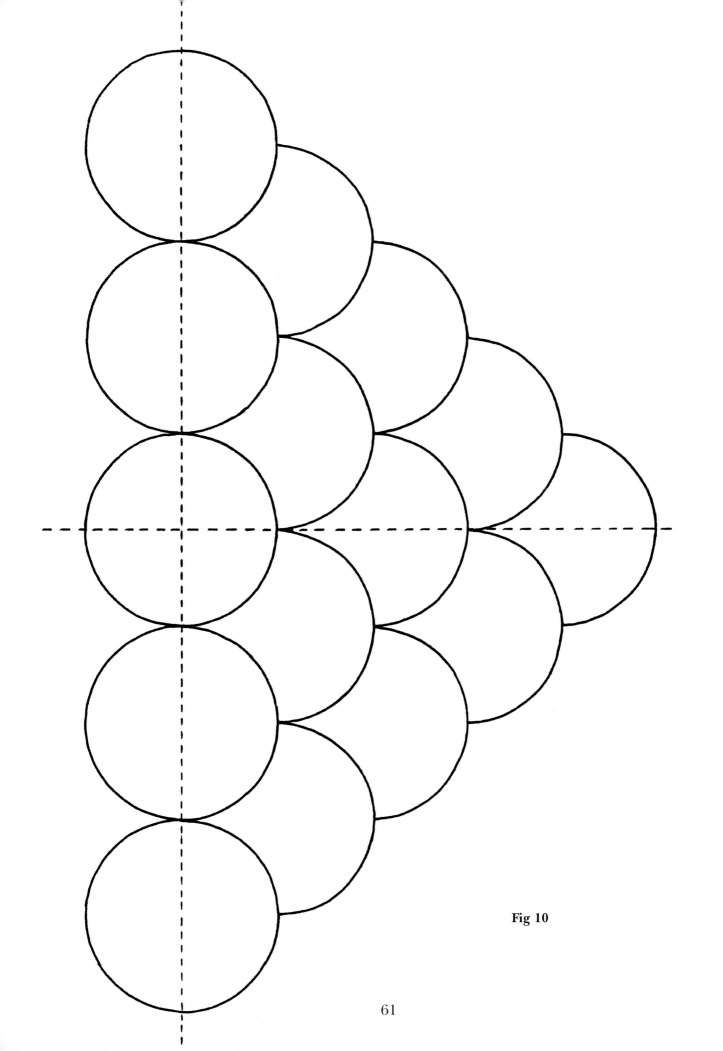

**Fig 10**

61

## JOYCE BOUCHER

*'I usually work with dark colours but for this quilt I decided to use paler fabrics. When making the first block the look did not seem right but I realised that the background cream and white leaf design helped to calm and blend, and after a few blocks the pale look I wanted came together.'*

thread to match the clamshell, not the background, stitch the folded curved edge in position using small, even slip stitches (Fig 12).

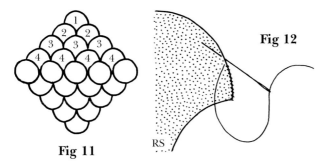

**Fig 11**

**Fig 12**

Once the clamshell's top edge is stitched, lift up the bottom edge of the fabric and ease the freezer paper out. Use a pair of scissors with rounded ends slid between the paper and the background fabric to separate them – the paper can then easily be pulled out. Try to remember to remove the paper *before* adding the next row of clamshells. It is very tiresome to remember only after the entire next row has been beautifully stitched in place. You *can* cut the background fabric away to remove the paper, which has to be done for the centre line of circles, but this is a lot more fiddly than just remembering to remove the papers directly the clamshells have been stitched down.

**9** Arrange the two clamshells that make the second row in position. The outer curves are placed on the drawn lines on the background and should overlap the bottom raw edges of the top clamshell by 1/4in (6mm). The two inner corners should meet midway on the stem of the top clamshell with all the bottom edges level as shown in Fig 13.

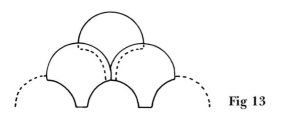

**Fig 13**

Iron both clamshells to fix their position on the background. Stitch the top curves in place, working right across the row. The stitching does not have to be through all the layers of fabric, just whatever is comfortable depending on the thickness of the fabrics. Once they have been stitched, remove both papers.

**10** Arrange the third row, overlapping the raw edges of the second row by 1/4in (6mm), following the drawn lines on the background fabric where

they can be seen (Fig 14). Press the row of clamshells with an iron to secure them and stitch along the top curves as before. If the colours of the clamshell fabrics vary in the row, change the thread to match each clamshell as you stitch it. I use a separate needle with each colour thread and use them in turn as I need them.

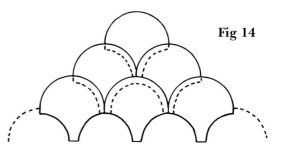

**Fig 14**

**11** Arrange, press and stitch the fourth row in the same way.
**12** Leave the centre row of circles. Turn the background fabric round and arrange and stitch the opposite four rows of clamshells in the design, beginning with the top single clamshell and working towards the centre.
**13** Position the five pressed circles so that they overlap the raw edges of both halves of the clamshell design, using the drawn lines on the background as a guide where they can be seen. Turn each circle so that the grain of the fabric runs parallel to the grain of the background before pressing them to fix them onto the block. Stitch each circle in place.
**14** Turn the block to the back and use the stitch lines as a guide to cut away the backing up to 1/4in (6mm) within the stitching lines of the circles, revealing the freezer paper below. Remove the freezer paper from the block (Fig 15).
**15** Trim the block to an exact 11 1/2in (29.2cm) square. Add the inner framing strips which should be 2in (5cm) wide strips. Trim the block to a 14in (35.6cm) square and add the sashing strips. See page 130 for adding framing strips and sashing.

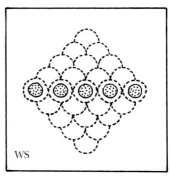

**Fig 15**

# FOLDED FLYING GEESE

This folded technique is a close relation of the Bow Tie technique used in another block in this sampler quilt. It uses rotary-cut squares and rectangles which are folded, layered and stitched to produce the Flying Geese design (Fig 1). The diagonal seams are not stitched but are folded pockets (Fig 2) which look very effective especially in a small size where piecing would be very fiddly.

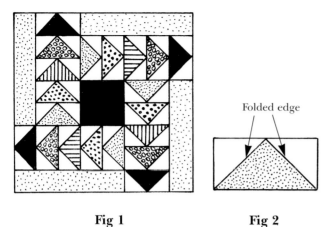

**Fig 1**

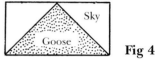

Folded edge

**Fig 2**

## COLOUR CHOICES

The design shown in Fig 1 has four lines of Flying Geese, each made up of five units. In my own arrangement (see picture page 2) I used five different fabrics in shades of blue grading from light to dark in the large triangles. This sequence of fabrics was repeated in each row of five Flying Geese. Alternative colour arrangements are shown in Figs 3a and 3b. Fig 3a uses four different fabrics for the larger triangles, one fabric for each row. Fig 3b uses two fabrics for the triangles in opposite rows. The same background fabric has been used for each Flying Geese unit and also for the outer long rectangles. Alternatively these long rectangles can be of another fabric as in Fig 1. The central square can

be a background fabric or a strong colour to make a central focus for the block.

## CONSTRUCTION

Each Flying Geese unit will measure 1½ x 3in (3.9 x 7.6cm) finished size. To make the block, twenty Flying Geese units must be assembled. For each unit you will need:
One rectangle 2 x 3½in (5 x 8.9cm) for the central triangle (called the 'goose' in the design);
Two squares each 2 x 2in (5 x 5cm) for the side triangles (called the 'sky') (Fig 4).

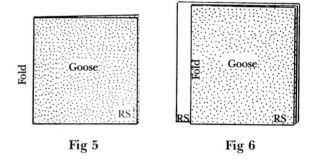

**Fig 4**

**1** From the chosen 'goose' fabric or fabrics, cut a total of twenty rectangles, one for each unit, each measuring 2 x 3½in (5 x 8.9cm). From the chosen 'sky' fabric, which acts as a background, cut forty squares each measuring 2 x 2in (5 x 5cm).
**2** Take one 'goose' rectangle and fold it in half with right side facing *outwards* (Fig 5). Place a square of 'sky' fabric down on a surface right side *up* and place the folded rectangle on the square, matching all the outer raw edges. You will find that the folded edge of the rectangle does not quite reach the edge of the square on the left-hand side (Fig 6).

**Fig 5**

**Fig 6**

**3** Place a second square of 'sky' fabric on the folded rectangle with right side *down*, matching the raw edges of the other 'sky' square exactly (Fig 7),

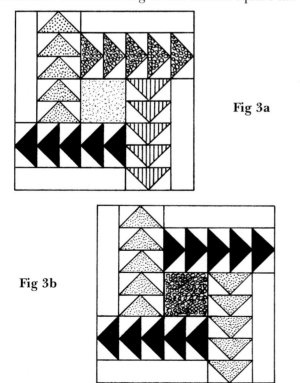

**Fig 3a**

**Fig 3b**

**Fig 7**

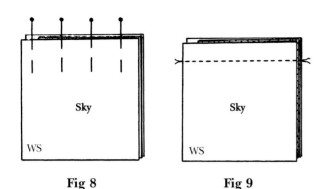

**Fig 8**　　　　　　　　**Fig 9**

then pin the top edges together (Fig 8). Machine a seam ¹/₄in (6mm) from the top edges through all the layers, including the fold of the rectangle (Fig 9).

**4** Pull the squares of 'sky' fabric back to reveal the centre folded rectangle (Fig 10). Then pull the corner of the rectangle marked A in Fig 10 across to meet the corner of the 'sky' also marked A. Pull the 'goose' corner marked B across to meet the corner of 'sky' marked B (Fig 11). Press the unit, ironing the central seam on the back *open* (Fig 12). Keep the large 'goose' triangle flat on the 'sky' with a couple of pins (Fig 13).

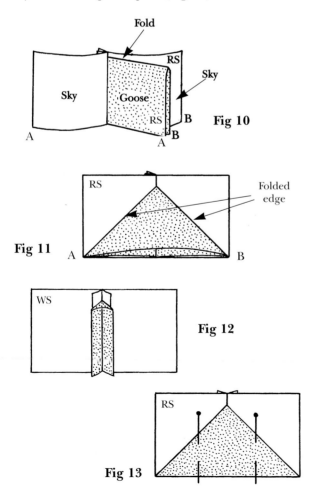

**Fig 10**

**Fig 11**

**Fig 12**

**Fig 13**

**5** Make all twenty Flying Geese units in this way, pressing and pinning each one as described.

**6** For the centre square in the block design, cut a square from the chosen fabric measuring 3¹/₂ x 3¹/₂in (8.9 x 8.9cm). For the side rectangles in the design cut four rectangles from the chosen fabric each measuring 2 x 8in (5 x 20.3cm).

**7** Arrange the Flying Geese units in four rows each containing five Flying Geese in the chosen colours (follow either Fig 1, Fig 3a or Fig 3b). Stitch the units into rows with the usual ¹/₄in (6mm) seam. Press the seams of the joined units towards the bottom of the row, ironing from the front of the work (Fig 14).

**8** Pin and stitch one long rectangle to the left side of each row of Flying Geese (Fig 15). Press the seam towards the long rectangle.

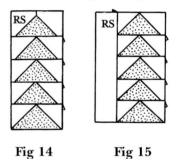

**Fig 14**　　　　　　　　**Fig 15**

**9** Arrange the four pieced sections of the block around the centre square as in Fig 1. To stitch these sections together by machine seems very difficult, but there is a clever way of dealing with it.

Begin by pinning the centre square to one pieced unit, right sides together, making sure that the square is pinned to the *bottom* two Flying Geese units with bottom edges level. The top edge of the centre square should extend ¹/₄in (6mm) above the seam between these two Flying Geese and the other three (Figs 16a and 16b). Stitch *part-way* along the pinned seam, leaving the top 1in (2.5cm) *unstitched* (Fig 17, page 68). Open the square out away from the pieced section, pressing the seam allowance towards the square (Fig 18).

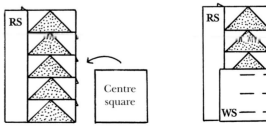

**Fig 16a**　　　　　　　　**Fig 16b**

### JUDY WALKER

*'Having opted for a new colour field, I had to give a great deal more thought to blending fabrics for each block. The challenge proved a great experience and I am very pleased with the result.'*

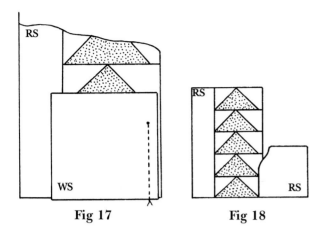

**Fig 17**　　　　**Fig 18**

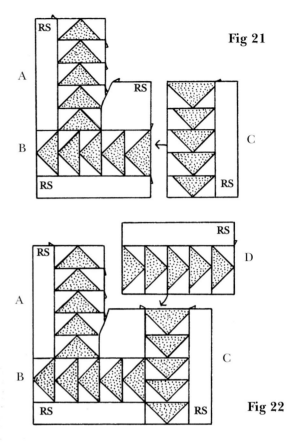

**Fig 21**

**10** Place the section back with the other pieces of the design (Fig 19). Pin and stitch section B to the main part of the block (section A plus the centre square), matching seams carefully. Press the seam towards the centre of the block (Fig 20).

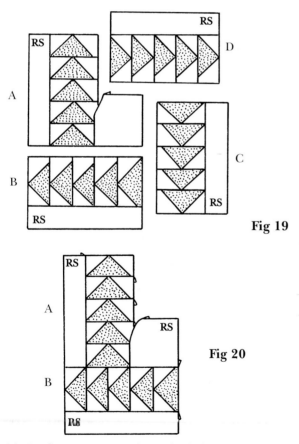

**Fig 19**

**Fig 22**

block, continuing the stitches of the original part-stitched seam.

**14** Press the block firmly from the front. It should measure $12^1/_2$ x $12^1/_2$in (31.7 x 31.7cm), but this is not essential. Add framing strips and trim the block to exactly 14 x 14in (35.6 x 35.6cm). Add sashing strips to complete the block (see page 130 for adding framing strips and sashing).

**Fig 20**

**11** In the same way, pin and stitch section C to the main block (Fig 21). Press the seam towards the centre of the block.
**12** Pin and stitch section D to the main block, as shown in Fig 22.
**13** Finally, pin and stitch the last seam of the

# REVERSE APPLIQUÉ

Reverse Appliqué is a technique much used in the short-sleeved shirts or waistcoats called molas made by the Kuna Indians from the San Blas Islands off the coast of Panama. It is also the basis of the designs stitched by the Hmong tribes from Laos, Vietnam and Thailand. Most of these ethnic designs use narrow channels of reverse appliqué to outline and decorate the shapes, which can be very geometric as in the Hmong designs, or may include animals and birds as do many molas. It is

also possible to stitch larger open areas as reverse appliqué, giving a similar effect to stencilling.

It is a misconception that reverse appliqué involves several layers of fabric tacked together and cut away to reveal the various colours. This would make a very bulky piece and could be very wasteful of fabric. It is better to tack fabric behind each area to be worked in reverse appliqué in turn, trimming off the excess after the appliqué has been completed.

In designing a block for this New Sampler Quilt I have steered away from the more ethnic channel-based designs and used the reverse appliqué technique in a circular design with a 1930s Art Deco feeling (Fig 1).

**Fig 1**

## COLOUR CHOICES

In conventional appliqué the pieces are stitched on to a background fabric. With reverse appliqué the main fabric is cut away to reveal the fabrics that make the design. What we have come to think of as the background to the design is used here as the foreground and becomes more dominant in the block. I continued my policy of using a neutral cream/beige shade wherever a background appeared in a block in my quilt, but this is not a firm ruling, just my personal choice.

Arrange the fabrics to be used in the design on the main foreground fabric to test their effect before beginning. As the appliqué is begun in the centre and worked outwards it is possible to change your mind about the fabrics as the design develops.

## CONSTRUCTION

**1** Cut a square of fabric for the main foreground 13½ x 13½in (34.3 x 34.3cm). Trace the *whole* design on to paper, using the parts of Fig 2 on pages 70, 71, 72 and 73, matching up the dotted lines and referring to Fig 1 if necessary. Mark the appliqué pattern on the *right* side of the foreground fabric square by tracing the design, using a sharp marking pencil and light box if necessary.

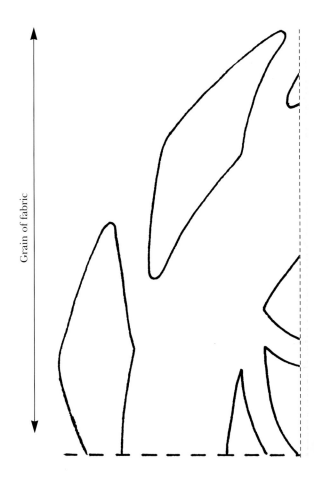

Grain of fabric

If the fabric is too dark for the design to be traced through, use dressmaker's carbon paper and a tracing wheel. (I use an empty fine ballpoint pen to mark the design through the carbon paper.) If the design is traced just *inside* the drawn line it will be hidden when the seam is turned under and stitched.

**2** Using a pair of sharp-pointed scissors, make a small snip in each part of the design that is going to be cut away (Fig 3). This makes it easier to cut the top layer away after the layers have been tacked together. I usually remember that I should have done this just as I finish tacking everything together. . . Do not cut any fabric away from the top layer at this stage.

**3** Take the fabric to be used as the centre flower and cut a piece large enough to cover the complete shape with at least ½in (1.2cm) to spare on

**Fig 3**

**Fig 2**
**top half**

CENTRE

all sides – about 4½ x 5½in (11.4 x 14cm) in size (Fig 4).

Pin the fabric on to the *back* of the main fabric, placing it *right* side against the main fabric and positioning it behind the drawn flower shape (Fig 5). Hold the two fabrics against a window or on a light box to check that the new piece of fabric is lying underneath the flower shape and extending at least ½in (1.2cm) beyond the drawn shape on all sides.

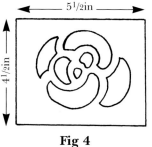

← 5½in →

4½in

**Fig 4**

**Fig 5**

Match the grain or weave of the second fabric with that of the main fabric square. Pin the layers together.
**4** With small stitches, about ¼in (6mm) in length, tack around each drawn shape ⅛–¼in (3–6mm) from the lines. Where the gap between two shapes is narrow, tack midway between the lines (Fig 6).

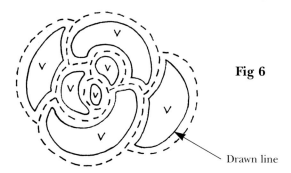

**Fig 6**

Drawn line

**5** Beginning with a large petal, slide the blade of a small pair of scissors through the little snipped area, between the layers of fabric and carefully cut away the top layer of fabric ⅛in (3mm) inside the drawn line (Fig 7). Only cut away each shape as you begin to stitch it so that the work stays stable.
**6** Concave curved edges may have to be clipped to help them turn under smoothly when being stitched. Do not clip right to the drawn line.

71

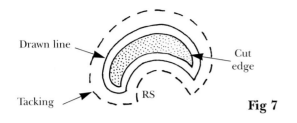

Drawn line

Tacking

Cut edge

RS

**Fig 7**

There's no need to clip convex curves. Clip right to the drawn line at any corners of the design (Fig 8).

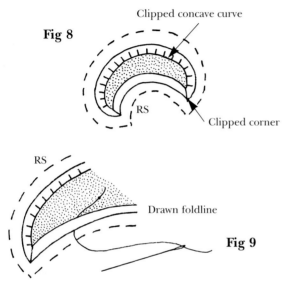

Clipped concave curve

**Fig 8**

RS

Clipped corner

RS

Drawn foldline

**Fig 9**

**7** Thread a fine appliqué needle (Sharps 10) with thread in a shade to match the top fabric. Begin with a knot and bring the needle up through the top layer of fabric on the marked line, hiding the knot between the fabrics (Fig 9). Begin midway along an edge, not at the corner. Corners are always tricky areas to deal with, so it is better to start well away from them and have established a good sewing rhythm by the time one is reached.
**8** Use the point of the needle to turn under the cut edge, stroking it under with the needle as you stitch. The drawn line should just disappear under the turned edge. Turn the cut edge under no more than 1/2in (1.2cm) ahead of the stitching as you work (Fig 10). Stitches should be about 1/10in (2mm) apart. Bring the needle up through the top layer of fabric close to the folded edge. Make the stitch by inserting the needle in the lower layer of fabric so that it is level with the thread on the top fabric and almost underneath the folded edge. The point should re-emerge in the folded edge about 1/10in (2mm) ahead of the first stitch (Fig 11). It is not a good idea to pin the fold under, as with only a 1/8in (3mm) turning, pins can cause the fabric to fray. Where the tacking has to be closer than 1/8in (3mm) to the drawn

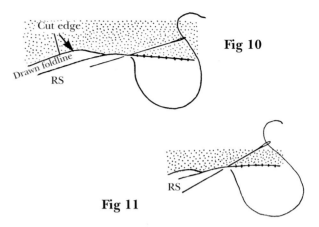

Cut edge

Drawn foldline

RS

**Fig 10**

RS

**Fig 11**

outline, just snip any tacking stitches that interfere with the turning process as you reach them.

Sharp corners present problems because there is so little fabric to tuck under. Cut right to the drawn corner and stitch as usual towards it, stroking the seam allowance cleanly under the fold line as you stitch. Stitch almost to the corner. Sew two stitches at the clipped corner itself, stitching into the top fabric *only* – this helps to prevent the

Grain of fabric

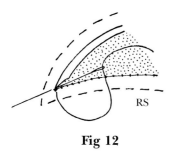

**Fig 12**

fabric from fraying (Fig 12). Sew one more stitch at the corner, this time also the underneath layer of fabric and continue to stitch away from the corner, turning the seam allowance under as you go. The first stitches should be very closely spaced, then easing back to the usual spacing as you work away from the corner.

**9** When the first petal of the flower has been completely stitched, choose another large petal and repeat the cutting and stitching process. If you leave the smallest and therefore the most fiddly shapes until last, you will have got used to the technique and will find them easier to handle.

**10** When the entire centre flower has been stitched, turn the block over and trim the excess

fabric around the design back to a scant 1/4in (6mm) beyond the stitches (Fig 13).

**11** The three pairs of leaves that join the centre flower can be treated as three separate areas or as one large unit. If you can spare the fabric, one piece of the chosen fabric can be cut and placed behind the design so that it extends at least 1/2in (1.2cm) beyond the leaves on all sides (Fig 14). A square of fabric cut 8 1/2 x 8 1/2in (21.6 x 21.6cm) will cover the area. However, if the fabric you want to use for the leaves is running low or you only

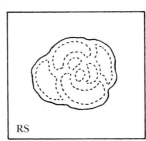

**Fig 13**

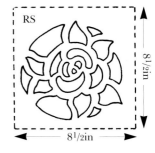

**Fig 14**

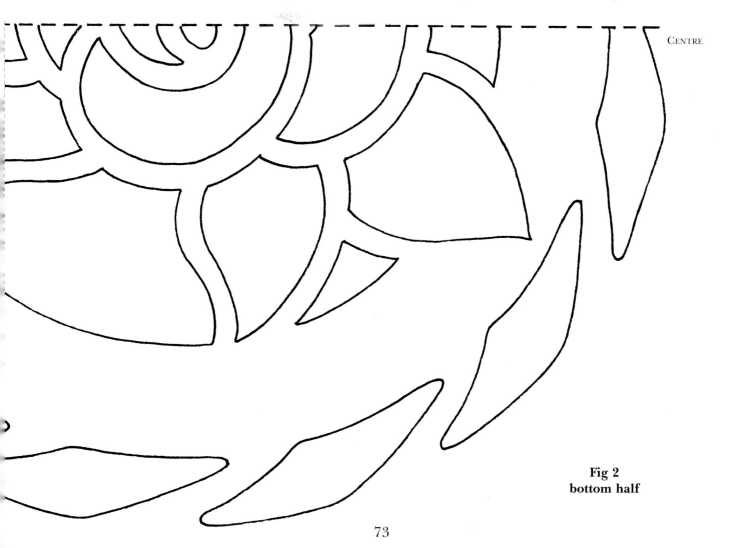

**Fig 2
bottom half**

### JEAN HALLS

*'During the Course I gradually turned a few metres of fabric into a
quilt. Because the blocks were busy, I decided to do a plain border, which
I feel makes a good frame for the quilt.'*

have small scraps, three pieces each about 4 x 5in (10 x 12.7cm) can be used instead (Fig 15).

**12** Pin the chosen fabric behind the drawn leaves on the main fabric square with right side against the back of the main fabric, following the method used for the centre flower. Take care to match the grain of the fabrics before tacking.

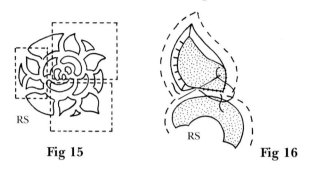

**Fig 15**                    **Fig 16**

Tack around each leaf shape, about ¹/8–¹/4in (3–6mm) outside each drawn shape. Cut away and stitch each leaf in turn. Where a leaf lies near a stitched petal, remove the tacking stitches as you sew, as the width of the top fabric between the petals and the leaves is very narrow (Fig 16). When all the leaves have been stitched, turn the block to the back and carefully cut away the excess fabric as before, leaving a scant ¹/4in (6mm) beyond the stitching line of each pair of leaves (Fig 17).

**Fig 17**

**13** For the inner circle that lies behind the flower and leaves, cut a piece of chosen fabric measuring 8¹/2 x 8¹/2in (21.6 x 21.6cm). Position it *right* side against the back of the main fabric square, matching the grain of both fabrics and pin in place. Tack around each section of the design as before. Cut and stitch each shape in turn. When all the shapes have been stitched, turn the block to its back and carefully cut away the excess fabric to a scant ¹/4in (6mm) beyond the stitching lines (Fig 18).

**14** The final twisted circle of the design needs a large piece of fabric I'm afraid, but if you cut away the excess carefully after stitching, you can preserve a good-sized circular piece from the centre

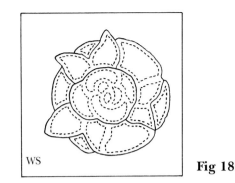

**Fig 18**

to use in another block. Cut a square of chosen fabric 12¹/2 x 12¹/2in (31.7 x 31.7cm) and pin and tack it behind the main block in the usual way. Cut and stitch each section in turn before flipping the block to the back and carefully trimming the excess fabric away from the *outside* of the circle, leaving it a scant ¹/4in (6mm) from the stitching lines (Fig 19).

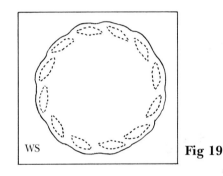

**Fig 19**

Carefully cut away the inner circle of excess fabric, leaving the fabric between the reverse appliqué shapes intact as the amount of fabric between the shapes is too narrow to cut away (Fig 20).

**15** Press the block and place on a cutting board. Trim it down to exactly 13 x 13in (33 x 33cm). Cut the inner framing strips 1in (2.5cm) wide and attach these (see page 130). Finally, add the sashing strips.

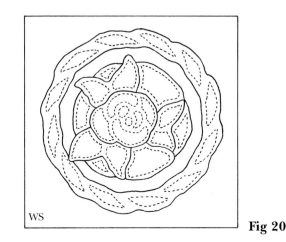

**Fig 20**

## MACHINE PIECED STRIP PATCHWORK

# BARGELLO

It is only recently that the term Bargello has been used in association with patchwork. It has traditionally been the name for Florentine canvas embroidery where parallel vertical straight stitches are worked in many subtle shadings of wool which rise or fall according to the pattern being followed. Each line of stitches is worked in a different shade from the one before to make curves or flame-like points. The principle of the technique is not unlike Seminole. Strips of fabric are joined into bands and

then cut vertically into pieces of varying widths. Narrow pieces result in steep curves in the design and wider pieces give gentler slopes (Fig 1).

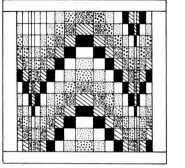

**Fig 1**

## COLOUR CHOICES

As the Bargello block needs to be a maximum size of around 13in (33cm) square, it is best to limit the number of fabrics to six. The idea is to shade the fabrics from light to dark. You may like to use just one colour shading, for instance from cream to fawn to ginger to dark brown in the six fabrics. It can be more interesting to use more than one colour, for instance, pale green through to dark forest green to dark grey up to pale silvery grey.

Put out all the fabrics you have to choose from and select any that you think might be useful. Arrange these side by side and overlapping so that you see just a strip of each one to give an idea of how a small amount relates to its neighbour. Do not limit yourself to six to start with. Once they are arranged you can weed out the less essential. Both prints and plains are fine to use, even very large prints as these become abstract when cut up and add interest to the design. Move the fabrics around until you are happy with the arrangement and aim for gentle shading rather than sharp contrasts.

## CONSTRUCTION

**1** From each of the six chosen fabrics cut *two* strips each 1¹/₂in (3.9cm) wide and 23in (58.4cm) long. If you cannot get strips as long as 23in (58.4cm), cut *four* strips that are each 1¹/₂in (3.9cm) wide and 13in (33cm) long from each fabric.
**2** Arrange the strips in the order that you intend using them. From left-over scraps, cut a small piece from each fabric (about 1in/2.5cm square) and stick them vertically on a piece of paper or card. Number each fabric as shown in Fig 2. You will need to refer to this chart as you work.
**3** Stitch each set of six strips together in the chosen order. Follow the guidelines for stitching together long strips given for the Seminole block

on page 19. You will have two identical bands of strips (four bands if you are using 13in (33cm) long strips). Do not press the bands yet.

Join the bands together to make one large piece, keeping the colours in the same repeat order (Fig 3). If you are using shorter strips, stitch the bands in pairs to make two pieces. Each will have the same arrangement of strips as in Fig 3.

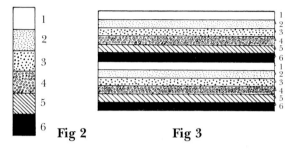

**Fig 2**          **Fig 3**

**4** Press the seams in alternate directions. Press lightly from the back to establish the directions of the seams and then flip the piece over and press firmly from the front. Make sure the seams are pulled open without folds or the strip widths will not be accurate.
**5** Place the piece on a flat surface and with the right side upwards as in Fig 3 bring the bottom strip (fabric 6) up so that it lies on the top strip (fabric 1) with right sides together and the long unstitched edges matching (Fig 4). Check that the piece is lying flat and not twisted, then pin. It does not matter if the side edges do not match – just that both layers of fabric are lying flat. Those using shorter strips will have *two* shorter tubes each with the same arrangement of strips as in Fig 3.

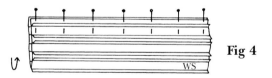

**Fig 4**

**6** Stitch the pinned seam to make a tube. Press the seam in whatever direction fits the alternating arrangement of seams in the rest of the band. Leave the tube with the seams on the outside as Fig 4.
**7** Place the tube of fabrics flat on a cutting board, lining the long top edges up with a horizontal marking on the board. Straighten one end, wasting as little fabric as possible. Now study the cutting chart in Fig 5, page 79. The first column gives all the information for the first piece to be cut. The top line shows the width of the piece to be cut, which is 1in (2.5cm). Cut the piece as in Fig 6.

What you have at this stage is a loop. The two

### HILARY BARKER

*'This second Sampler Quilt enabled me to fulfil a desire to use blue and white fabrics. The intricate and interesting blocks were a joy to work on, with the added bonus of wintry scenes appearing when they were completed. The Flying Geese border helped to use up some of the left-overs.'*

**Fig 5**

| WIDTH OF STRIP | 1in 2.5 cm | 1in 2.5 cm | ³/4in 1.9 cm | ³/4in 1.9 cm | 1in 2.5 cm | 1in 2.5 cm | 1¼in 3.2 cm | 1¼in 3.2 cm | 1½in 3.8 cm | 2in 5 cm | 1½in 3.8 cm | 1¼in 3.2 cm | 1¼in 3.2 cm | 1in 2.5 cm | 1in 2.5 cm | ³/4in 1.9 cm | ³/4in 1.9 cm | 1in 2.5 cm | 1in 2.5 cm |
|---|---|---|---|---|---|---|---|---|---|---|---|---|---|---|---|---|---|---|---|
| TOP FABRIC | 1 | 6 | 5 | 4 | 5 | 6 | 1 | 2 | 3 | 4 | 3 | 2 | 1 | 6 | 5 | 4 | 5 | 6 | 1 |
| BOTTOM FABRIC | 6 | 5 | 4 | 3 | 4 | 5 | 6 | 1 | 2 | 3 | 2 | 1 | 6 | 5 | 4 | 3 | 4 | 5 | 6 |

other rows in the chart column tell you where the seam must be undone to convert the loop into a Seminole-type piece. For the first piece the top fabric is no.1 and the bottom is no.6. They occur twice in the loop, but just locate one pair and ignore the other.

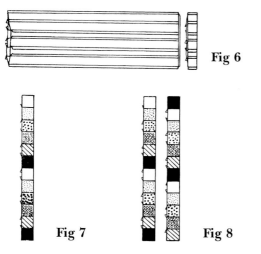

**Fig 6**

**Fig 7**      **Fig 8**

Hold fabric 1 in your left hand and fabric 6 in your right and undo the seam that joins them. Pin the piece on a board or lay it out on a clear surface with fabric 1 at the top and fabric 6 at the bottom (Fig 7). Tick the first column on the chart to show that you have dealt with that piece.

**8** Cut piece 2, which is also 1in (2.5cm) wide. Find fabrics 6 and 5 next to each other in the loop. Hold fabric 6 in one hand and fabric 5 in the other hand and undo the seam that joins them. Place the second piece next to the first piece with fabric 6 at the top and fabric 5 at the bottom, working from left to right (Fig 8). Tick the second column on the chart in Fig 5 once you have done this.

**9** Continue to cut each piece in turn, following the width measurements from the chart. The pattern of curves and steps develop as the pieces are unstitched and placed next to each other. The V-shaped symbols on the chart show where the slope comes to a peak or a valley. The slope descends through four pieces and then climbs to a broad peak in the centre of the block. It then descends and rises

as a mirror image of the first half (see Fig 1).

**10** When all the pieces have been cut and arranged, begin pinning and stitching them together. The narrower the pieces, the more tricky it is to stitch them, so begin in the centre and work out to one side: that way you will have had some experience of the stitching process before you hit the really narrow pieces. The pinning and stitching is very similar to Seminole.

To join, place the two strips right sides together and stitch lengthwise, matching seams carefully. The initial pressing of the seams in alternate directions means that the seams will lock together so you can stitch without pinning if you want to. The experience of making the Seminole block will have shown you just how much pinning you need to do. Remember, there are no rules. If you feel you need to pin each junction before you stitch, then do so. Take particular care to match seams where there are definite changes in colour as any inaccuracies will show up here. In other areas where the fabrics are more subtly shaded, a mismatched seam will not notice at all. Wait until the whole block is pieced before making a decision to re-stitch a seam, as you may well find that it has merged in with the design and really doesn't notice at all. Press the seams from the front to one side before adding each new piece as this makes it easier to handle.

**11** Once all the pieces are joined, the block needs to be pressed from the front and placed on a cutting board to check its size. Some of the pieces, especially the very narrow ones, will probably look uneven in width. Use a steam iron to get them pulled out as evenly as possible. Aim to finish up with a reasonably rectangular or square block, never mind the actual measurements. Trim the top and bottom edges to straighten them, but use the steam iron and some judicious pulling to get the sides straight. Measure the block from top to bottom and from side to side. It doubtless won't measure the same, so just add wider framing strips on the shorter sides. Trim the block to an exact 14in (35.6cm) square and then add the sashing strips (see page 130).

# PINEAPPLE

The Pineapple design is a close relative of Log Cabin, using strips stitched around a centre square. The main difference is that the strips in the Pineapple are not just stitched in a square around the centre but also at 45° to the centre, making a more complex eight-sided design (Fig 1).

Traditionally the design has been drawn onto a foundation fabric like calico and the strips stitched to this, using the drawn lines as guidelines. More recently, specialist Pineapple rulers have made the

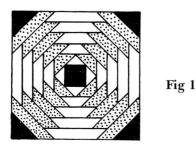

**Fig 1**

task easier and quicker, although there is less control over the general accuracy and joining many blocks together for a quilt often means a good deal of fudging. The Pineapple block for this New Sampler Quilt is made using the foundation piecing technique which is so popular at present.

## COLOUR CHOICES

The block uses two alternating colours for the strips with a third in the centre and the final corners. A variety of different fabrics in each colour can be used for the strips or just two fabrics throughout the block. The centre can be a contrasting fabric or one that tones more subtly with the two main fabrics. Decisions on the fabric for the

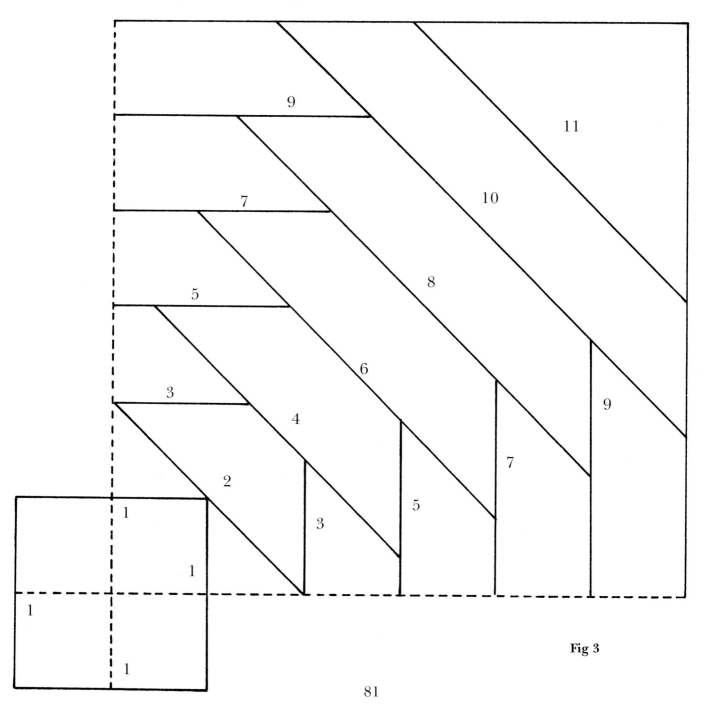

**Fig 3**

corners can be left until that stage in the design is reached when it is easier to make the right choice.

### Working with a Foundation

The foundation or base on which the design is drawn and to which the fabrics are stitched can be one that is removed once the block is completed, like paper or a woven tear-away foundation, or one that is left permanently in place like calico. For the Pineapple block in this quilt it is better to use a foundation that can be removed afterwards so the block has the same thickness and flexibility as the others in the quilt. It helps to be able to see through the foundation, so tracing paper or freezer paper are both excellent, or a woven tear-away foundation which can be purchased from fabric shops.

### Preparing for Sewing

Stitching along a drawn line on a foundation is easier if an open-front foot is used on the machine so you can see both needle and line as you stitch. Use a larger size 90/14 needle as this makes larger holes in the foundation, making it easier to remove. For the same reason, reduce the stitch length to about 18–20 stitches to the inch. Do a test run on a measured inch on some fabric and count the stitches to find the correct setting for your machine.

## CONSTRUCTION

**1** Cut a square of foundation such as tracing paper, freezer paper or a tear-away woven foundation measuring 12½ x 12½in (31.7 x 31.7cm). Fold it lightly into four quarters (Fig 2).

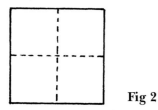

**Fig 2**

**2** Trace the design shown in Fig 3 (page 81) on to one quarter of the foundation, matching the dotted lines in Fig 3 with the folds in the foundation (Fig 4). Number the lines as in Fig 3. Turn the foundation and position a second quarter over the design in Fig 3, matching the dotted lines and folds as before. Trace the design on to the foundation and add the numbers. Repeat this in the remaining two sections of the foundation to complete the full Pineapple design, as seen in Fig 1.

**3** From the fabric chosen for the centre square cut a square measuring 2½ x 2½in (6.3 x 6.3cm).

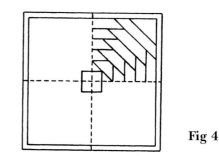

**Fig 4**

From the fabrics chosen for the two main colours cut strips 1½in (3.9cm) wide. A total of about 110in (2.79m) of strip is needed for the strips that run out towards the sides of the block (shown as white in Fig 1). A total of about 120in (3.05m) of strip is needed for the strips that are set at 45° and run towards the corners of the block (shown shaded in Fig 1). If you are using several different fabrics, cut them for each round of strips as you go.

**4** Place the centre square of fabric right side *up* on the unmarked side of the foundation (this is the front) over the drawn centre square on the design so that it overlaps the drawn square by ¼in (6mm) on all sides. If you cannot see too well through the foundation, hold it up against the light on the sewing machine. Pin the square in position (Fig 5).

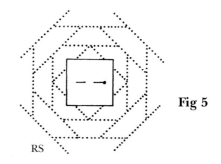

**Fig 5**

RS

**5** To make Round One, from the fabric chosen for the strips shown as white in Fig 1 cut four pieces each 2½in (6.3cm) long. Place one piece on the pinned square, right sides facing, with the edges matching (Fig 6). Pin in position, keeping

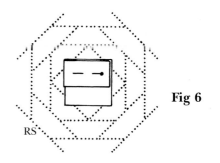

**Fig 6**

RS

the pin well away from the seam allowance where the stitching will be. Turn the foundation over to the drawn side (the back of the block). The numbers show the order of stitching. Stitch along the drawn line marked 1 through both thicknesses of fabric, extending two or three stitches beyond the beginning and end of the drawn line (Fig 7).

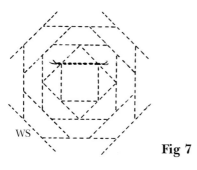

**Fig 7**

**6** Turn to the right side and trim the seam allowance down to a scant ¹/₄in (6mm) by eye with a pair of sharp scissors. Flip the strip over on to the foundation, finger press the seam and press with an iron from the front of the work (Fig 8).

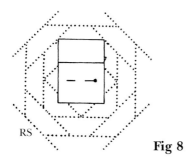

**Fig 8**

**7** Repeat this process with a second piece of fabric on the opposite side of the centre square. Press it over on to the foundation as before (Fig 9).

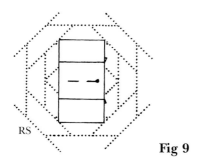

**Fig 9**

**8** In the same way pin and stitch the remaining two pieces to the other sides of the centre square. Press over on to the foundation (Fig 10).
**9** Cut four pieces from a strip of the second fabric (the shaded strips in Fig 1), each 3¹/₂in (8.9cm)

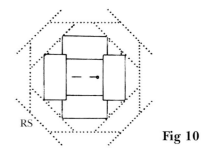

**Fig 10**

long. These will make Round Two of the design. It is not easy to position these strips in the correct place on the front of the block because the line is masked by the fabric already stitched to the foundation. It helps to trim the stitched lengths down at this stage. Turn the foundation to the marked side and place a thin ruler along the next stitching line (marked 2 on the foundation). Pull the foundation back along this line against the edge of the ruler. Do not worry if the foundation pulls away from the stitches at the ends of the seams. Trim the fabric by eye to a scant ¹/₄in (6mm) beyond the folded edge of the foundation (Fig 11). Do this on all four sides on each line marked 2 on the foundation (Fig 12).

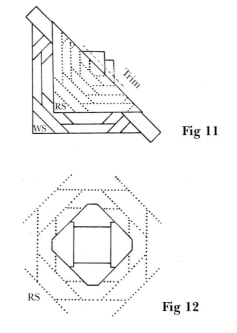

**Fig 11**

**Fig 12**

**10** Position one cut strip of the second fabric on one of the trimmed sides of the block with right sides facing, lining up the edges. Pin in position and turn the foundation over to the marked side. Stitch along the drawn line marked 2 through both layers of fabric, sewing two or three stitches beyond the drawn line at the start and finish.

## GILL SMITH

*'The start of my second Sampler Quilt coincided with my daughter's engagement, so I decided to make it as a wedding present. Hence the four extra quilted pictures depicting places special to Wendy and James, the fourth being the church where they were to be married. It was finished just in time!'*

Turn to the right side and flip the fabric over on to the foundation. Press into position with an iron.

Repeat this with a second cut strip on the opposite side of the block and then the other two cut strips, pressing each strip out on to the foundation as they are stitched.

**11** Trim the excess fabric from the block by turning the foundation to the drawn side and placing a ruler along each line marked 3. Pull the foundation back against the edge of the ruler and trim the fabric to a scant $\frac{1}{4}$in (6mm) beyond the folded edge of the foundation (Fig 13).

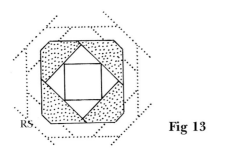

**Fig 13**

**12** From a strip of the first fabric (shown as white in Fig 1) cut four pieces each $3\frac{3}{4}$in (9.5cm) long. Pin and stitch them to each side of the block, stitching along the drawn lines marked 3 on the foundation. This makes Round Three of the design. Flip each piece over and press on to the foundation. Use a ruler placed on the lines marked 4 to trim the fabric down as before. You will find that as the block progresses gaps appear between the pieces of fabric along each edge and you may not need to trim the fabric back to be able to position the next round of strips accurately. Just do whatever makes it easiest for you.

**13** The next round of strips (Round Four) uses four pieces of the second fabric each $4\frac{1}{2}$in (11.4cm) long. Stitch these to the foundation as before.

**14** Continue to build out the block, stitching four strips each time along the marked lines. The length of strip used each time is as follows:
Round Five: four strips of fabric 1, each $4\frac{1}{2}$in (11.4cm) long.
Round Six: four strips of fabric 2, each $5\frac{1}{4}$in (13.3cm) long.
Round Seven: four strips of fabric 1, each $5\frac{1}{4}$in (13.3cm) long.
Round Eight: four strips of fabric 2, each $6\frac{1}{4}$in (15.9cm) long.
Round Nine: four strips of fabric 1, each $6\frac{1}{4}$in (15.9cm) long.
Round Ten: four strips of fabric 2, each 7in (17.8cm) long.

**15** For the final corners of the block cut two squares from the chosen fabric each measuring $4\frac{1}{4}$ x $4\frac{1}{4}$in (10.8 x 10.8cm). These are slightly larger than necessary, but it is better to have a little extra to trim down to the final size.

Cut each square diagonally to make the four corners. Pin the longest edge of each triangle to the corners of the block, right sides facing, and stitch along the drawn lines marked 11 on the foundation (Fig 14). Press the corners back on to the foundation.

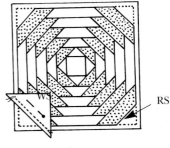

**Fig 14**

**16** Trim the block and foundation to exactly $\frac{1}{4}$in (6mm) beyond the outer drawn line (Fig 15). This makes a block $12\frac{1}{2}$ x $12\frac{1}{2}$in (31.7 x 31.7cm).

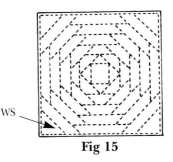

**Fig 15**

**17** It is a good idea to add the framing strips to the block while the foundation is still in place as it adds stability and the stitching line is marked ready for use. Cut framing strips, two measuring $1\frac{1}{4}$ x $12\frac{1}{2}$in (3.2 x 31.7cm) and two $1\frac{1}{4}$ x 14in (3.2 x 35.6cm). Pin and stitch the two shorter strips to the sides of the block, stitching along the drawn line on the foundation. Press the seams outwards away from the block, pressing from the front of the work. Pin and stitch the two longer strips to the top and bottom of the block in the same way. Press seams outwards from the front of the block.

**18** Turn the block to the back and carefully remove all the paper foundation. Finally, add the sashing strips to the block (see page 130).

# ATTIC WINDOWS

T he Attic Windows block has long been a favourite for quilters because of its three-dimensional effect. Each square is made from three pieces that when assembled give an impression of a window with the front window-sill and one side of the frame. When a number of these are joined together the effect becomes that of a large window divided up into smaller panes (Fig 1). This illusion is created by using the same fabric throughout for the horizontal window-sills and another fabric for

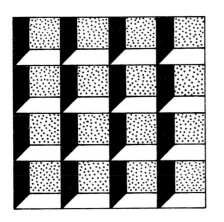

**Fig 1**

all the side window frames. By making one of these sets of strips in a light fabric and the other in a darker fabric, the three-dimensional effect is enhanced.

## COLOUR CHOICE

Although the piecing technique for Attic Windows is straightforward, I have left the block until this later stage in the sequence of techniques because by now you will have had plenty of experience in selecting and balancing fabrics which should help when you start sorting out the choices for this block.

First, choose two fabrics for the window-sills and window frames, one light and one dark. It does not matter which you use horizontally for the window-sills and which for the vertical window frames, so arrange them together and make your decision by seeing how they look before cutting anything.

The fabric squares used for the windows themselves give an opportunity to create a design that is absolutely unique. A variety of fabrics can be used to paint a picture through the windows: I used varying blues shading from light in one corner to dark in the opposite corner to give the feeling of a night sky. A whole garden scene or townscape could be created by careful selection of sections of fabrics that are cut to size and arranged across the block. You have sixteen windows to play with, four in each row, so there is plenty of scope for enjoying yourself with the design.

If this seems too intimidating then look for windows that create the feeling of depth to accentuate the three-dimensional effect of the block. This may be just one solid fabric or a series of subtly graded shades. Lay out your fabrics and ponder it. Do not rush things: the cutting and piecing are the easy bits, it is the agonising over the choice of window fabrics that takes the time.

The squares for the windows are 2 x 2in (5 x

5cm) finished size, and it is a good idea to make the template in clear plastic so that you can move it across the fabric and find the most effective sections to cut out and use. This is one design where a pin-board is a great help. Cut out all the separate pieces and pin them in place on the board. Place the board vertically and stand well back so that you can consider the effect. Rearrange or even re-cut pieces if necessary. Once all this agonising is done, make a note of the final arrangement before you dismantle it to stitch it.

## CONSTRUCTION

Templates A and B in Fig 2 are for traditional American Piecing. The templates are drawn around on the back of the fabric and the shapes cut out with a 1/4in (6mm) seam allowance added on all sides. The drawn lines are the stitching lines and may be stitched by hand or by machine.

Template C (Fig 14, page 89) has seam allowances already added and can be used for an alternative machine-pieced method, described on page 89.

### *Traditional Piecing Method*

**1** Make the templates, preferably from clear template plastic, by tracing the two shapes from Fig 2. Mark the directional arrows as these show how the templates should be positioned on the grain or weave of the fabric.

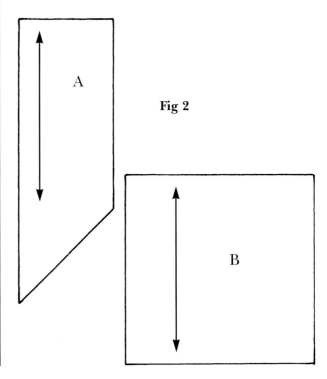

**Fig 2**

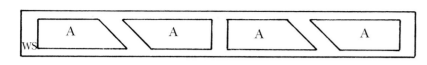

Fig 3

**2** From the fabric to be used for the window-sills (the horizontal strips in the design) cut a strip measuring $1\frac{1}{2}$ x 52in (3.9 x 132cm). Several shorter strips can be used if you do not have this length in one piece. Use rotary cutting equipment to cut the strips.

From the fabric to be used for the window frames (the vertical strips in the design) cut a similar strip measuring $1\frac{1}{2}$ x 52in (3.9 x 132cm). Again, shorter strips can be used if you do not have this length in one piece.

**3** Lay the window-sill strip with *wrong* side uppermost on a cutting board. Draw round template A with a sharp marking pencil sixteen times, leaving a $\frac{1}{4}$in (6mm) seam allowance at the top and bottom edges and allowing at least $\frac{1}{2}$in (1.2cm) between each drawn outline so that the seam allowance of $\frac{1}{4}$in (6mm) can be added to each shape when cutting out. Save space by arranging the templates as in Fig 3. Make sure that the template looks *exactly* like that in Fig 3 – do not flip the template over or the design will not work.

**4** Cut out each shape to include the $\frac{1}{4}$in (6mm) seam allowance, either by eye or by using a rotary cutter and ruler. The top and bottom edges are already cut as they are the edges of the fabric strip, so it is just the sides that need to be cut (Fig 4).

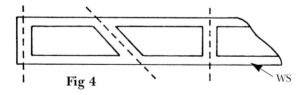

**Fig 4**

**5** Take the cut strip of fabric chosen for the window frames. The same template A must first be *reversed*. Turn it over completely so that the slanted edge is facing the opposite way to when it was used previously. If you do not do this, the piecing of the Attic Window is impossible: you will have the equivalent of two left sleeves!

Using the reversed template A (Fig 5) repeat the process of marking and cutting the strip as for

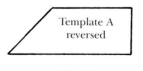

Template A reversed

**Fig 5**

the window-sill pieces. You should finish up with sixteen pieces of one fabric for the window-sills and sixteen pieces of the other fabric for the window frames (Fig 6).

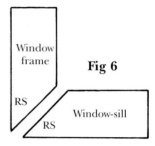

Window frame

RS

Window-sill

RS

**Fig 6**

**6** If you are choosing specific sections of a piece of fabric for the windows you may need to look and mark on the *right* side of the fabric. To do this make an extra window template in clear plastic that measures $2\frac{1}{2}$ x $2\frac{1}{2}$in (6.3 x 6.3cm) to include the seam allowances. Use this to find the exact part of the design that you want. Draw round it on the *right* side of the fabric and cut out exactly on the drawn line. Turn the square of fabric over and position template B on the *back* of the fabric leaving a $\frac{1}{4}$in (6mm) seam allowance on all sides. Draw round template B to give the stitching line on the fabric (Fig 7).

If you do *not* need to look at the right side of the fabric when marking and cutting the window squares, use template B only. On the *wrong* side of the chosen fabric draw accurately around the template sixteen times using a sharp marking pencil and matching the direction of the arrow with the grain of the fabric as usual. Allow at least $\frac{1}{2}$in (1.2cm) between each drawn outline so that the seam allowances of $\frac{1}{4}$in (6mm) can be added to each shape when cutting out (Fig 8). Cut out each

WS

**Fig 7**

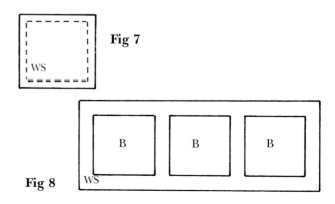

B  B  B

WS

**Fig 8**

square to include the ¼in (6mm) seam allowance.
**7** Arrange each Attic Window as in Fig 9 and pin them on a board to check the effect of your arrangement.

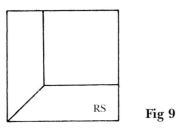

**Fig 9**

### Stitching the Units

Follow step 8 if stitching the units by hand, or steps 9–13 if stitching by machine.

#### Stitching by Hand

**8** To hand-piece the units, place the window square and one of the side strips right sides together along the two sides to be joined (Fig 10). Pin and stitch along the marked lines, following the method used for piecing the Tangled Star block (page 26), known as American Piecing. Do not stitch beyond the marked corners into the seam allowances (Fig 11).

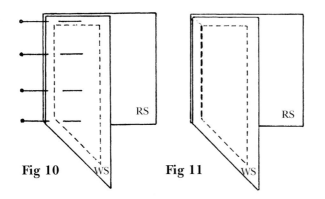

**Fig 10**    **Fig 11**

In the same way pin and stitch the other side strip to the square, stitching only to the marked corners of the design (Fig 12). Finally, pin and

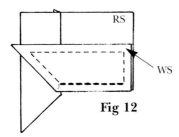

**Fig 12**

stitch the last seam, working from the inner corner where the side pieces meet the window square towards the outer corner. Push the seam allowances away from the stitching line and begin by matching the marked corner on both side pieces only, avoiding any fabric of the window square (Fig 13).

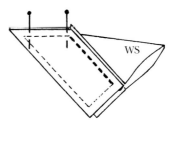

**Fig 13**

#### Stitching by Machine

**9** If you intend to machine-piece this block you may like to cut the pieces with the seam allowances already added on. Template C in Fig 14 is for the bottom sill and side frame of the windows with the ¼in (6mm) seam allowance already added.

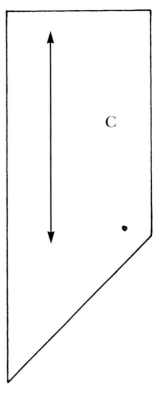

**Fig 14**

## MARIAN CHINERY

*'The fabrics for this quilt came from America, Canada and England, while the wool wadding came from New Zealand. A lot of the quilting was done on holiday in different places. It really should be called "Trip Around the World".'*

Cut strips as for the hand-piecing technique. Place the template on the wrong side of the strip for the window-sill. The top and bottom edges should match the edges of the fabric strip. Draw along the other two edges of the template (Fig 15).

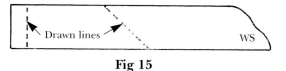

**Fig 15**

Turn the template round and place it so that the drawn slanted line on the fabric exactly lines up with the slanted edge of the template. Draw along the straight side of the template (Fig 16). Repeat this process along the strip of fabric until sixteen shapes have been marked. Using a rotary cutter and ruler cut exactly along each drawn line to give sixteen window-sill pieces.

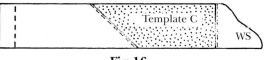

**Fig 16**

**10** Turn template C over and repeat the process on the strip cut for the window frames to give sixteen shapes.

**11** For the window, cut sixteen squares of fabric each measuring $2^{1}/_{2}$ x $2^{1}/_{2}$in (6.3 x 6.3cm). You may need to use a plastic template to draw round if you are choosing particular areas of fabric, otherwise cut a strip $2^{1}/_{2}$ (6.3cm) wide and cut squares from it, each measuring $2^{1}/_{2}$ x $2^{1}/_{2}$in (6.3 x 6.3cm).

**12** On the *wrong* side of each window square draw a dot at the bottom right corner $^{1}/_{4}$in (6mm) in from both edges to mark the stitching corner. Do the same at the inner stitching corner on each side strip (Fig 17).

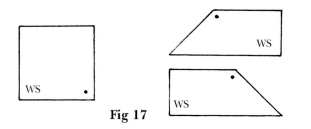

**Fig 17**

**13** Pin and stitch one side strip as shown in Fig 18, matching the marked dots and stitching a $^{1}/_{4}$in (6mm) seam. Do not stitch beyond the marked

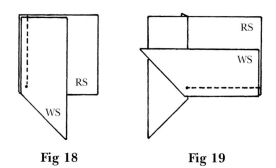

**Fig 18**          **Fig 19**

dots into the seam allowance. In the same way pin and stitch the other side strip (Fig 19). Finally, pin and stitch the last seam, stitching from the marked dots towards the outer corner (Fig 20).

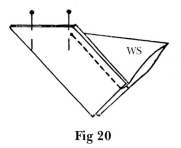

**Fig 20**

Push all the seam allowances and window fabric away from the seam so that they are not caught in the stitching. This seam is on the bias, so try not to pull and stretch it as you stitch.

### *Assembling the Units*

**14** Assemble all the sixteen units in your chosen method. Press each unit from the front, pressing the seam allowances away from the window square and the diagonal seam allowances to one side.

**15** Place the stitched and pressed units in the chosen arrangement. Join the units into horizontal rows, pinning and matching the seams and stitching either by hand or by machine.

If sewing by hand, leave the seam allowances unstitched and press only after the whole block has been assembled. If stitching by machine, press the seams from the front, ironing the seams of row one in one direction, those of row two the opposite way and so on. Join the rows together, matching the seams carefully. Press the completed block from the front of the work.

**16** The block should now measure $12^{1}/_{2}$ x $12^{1}/_{2}$in (31.7 x 31.7cm). Add the inner framing strips of a cut width of $1^{1}/_{4}$in (3.2cm) to bring the block up to 14 x 14in (35.6 x 35.6cm). Finally, add the sashing strips. See page 130 for adding framing strips and sashing.

# MONKEY WRENCH

When I first began teaching the original Sampler Quilt course I included the block Monkey Wrench (Fig 1), but ceased to use it after a while as it seemed too simple a design and slightly out of scale with the other blocks in the quilt. Later

I realised that it needed to be used as a repeat design with four smaller versions put together to make one block so that the circular movement of the colours could be seen (Fig 2). This block has great potential for a design used throughout a

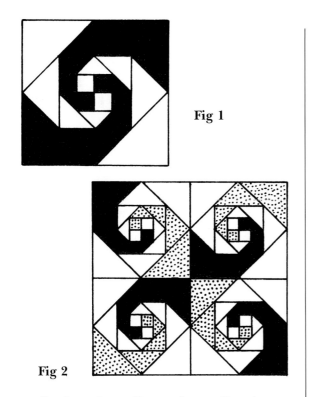

Fig 1

Fig 2

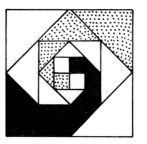

Fig 3

larger quilt where the curling and uncurling shapes can be exploited.

Because each Monkey Wrench block measures only 6 x 6in (15.2 x 15.2cm), it is most accurately and successfully pieced using the foundation technique where the design is traced onto paper, Vilene, a woven tear-away foundation or even calico. The fabric pieces are placed onto the unmarked side of the foundation and stitched in place along the lines marked on the back of the foundation. This makes the piecing very accurate and keeps the block stable as you work. Once the four blocks are completed they will all measure exactly the same size and can be joined together without the usual 'easing and adjusting' that is part and parcel of quilt-making.

I have described foundation piecing as a machine technique, but it can just as easily be stitched by hand. A firm foundation that will stay permanently behind the block, such as calico or a fine Vilene, is best for hand-work, as pulling paper away from hand-stitching can strain the stitches.

## COLOUR CHOICES
The Monkey Wrench block (Fig 1) consists of four curving shapes that spiral out from the centre. Just two fabrics can be used in the opposite spirals as in Fig 1 or three fabrics as in Fig 3. For my quilt (see page 2) I used two of my blue fabrics for opposing spirals with the other two in a background fabric.

### Working with a Foundation
Two types of foundation can be used for this work: one that is removed after the block has been completed, like paper, tracing paper or a woven tear-away foundation; or one that is left behind the block to give it stability, like Vilene or calico. Using a permanent foundation does eliminate the tedious task of pulling all the paper from the block once it is finished but will make the block thicker and heavier, especially if calico is used. I prefer a fine Vilene which can be left in position without adding thickness and is also virtually transparent, a great help when piecing.

For the Monkey Wrench block in this New Sampler quilt I would recommend a foundation that can be removed afterwards so that the block has the same weight and flexibility as the others in the quilt. It does help to be able to see through the foundation, so tracing paper or freezer paper are both excellent, or you can buy a woven tear-away foundation from fabric shops.

### Using the Fabrics
Most projects using foundation piecing are very vague about the fabric: just cut pieces larger than you need is often all the advice they give. Because this block is repeated four times and also because most of the pieces are right-angled triangles I have estimated generously the size of triangles needed to cover each piece and given specific measurements to be cut. This will save on fabric and also will get you used to working on a foundation reasonably painlessly.

### Preparing for Sewing
To make it easier to stitch exactly on the drawn line on the foundation, an open-front foot is needed for this technique so that you get a good view of both the line and the needle. The 1/4in foot for most machines does this job nicely, or you can cut the centre part out of a plastic foot. I used a hacksaw from a child's toolbox to do this with great success. Change the needle in your machine from the usual 80/12 to a larger 90/14 – this makes larger holes in

the paper so that it can be removed more easily. The stitch length should be set even smaller than usual, approximately 18–20 stitches to the inch, for the same reason. Do a test run on a measured inch on some fabric and count the stitches so you will know the correct setting for your own machine.

## CONSTRUCTION

**1** Cut four pieces of foundation such as tracing paper, freezer paper or a tear-away woven foundation, each measuring 7 x 7in (17.8 x 17.8cm). Trace the Monkey Wrench block, shown in Fig 4 below, carefully on to each foundation, using a ruler and sharp pencil, keeping all the lines as accurate as possible. Also trace the numbers shown on the block.

**2** If *three* fabrics are being used for the block (two fabrics plus a background) as in Fig 3, measure and cut one set of the following squares from *each* fabric, *plus* an extra set in the background fabric as it's being used twice in the design:
two squares 2¹/4 x 2¹/4in (5.7 x 5.7cm);
two squares 2³/4 x 2³/4in (7 x 7cm);
two squares 3¹/2 x 3¹/2in (8.9 x 8.9cm);
two squares 4¹/2 x 4¹/2in (11.4 x 11.4cm).

If only *two* fabrics are being used as in Fig 1 cut *two* sets of squares (four squares of each size) from each fabric.

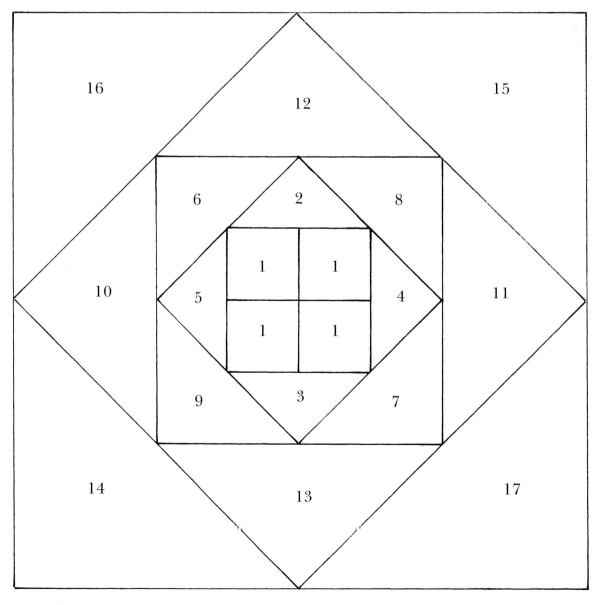

**Fig 4**

**3** Cut all the squares in half diagonally to make triangles (Fig 5). Sort these into piles of each size and colour ready to use.

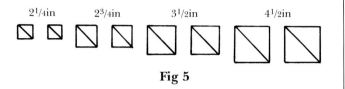

**Fig 5**

**4** The four-patch in the centre of each block is constructed separately and placed on the foundation. If *three* fabrics are being used, cut one strip from each main fabric and two strips from the background fabric. Each strip should measure 1¼ x 6in (3.2 x 15.2cm). Stitch the strips into pairs (Fig 6). Press the seams towards the darker fabrics.

If only *two* fabrics are being used, cut two strips of each fabric, then stitch the strips into pairs and press as above (Fig 6).

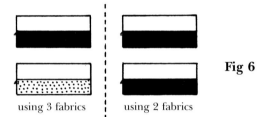

using 3 fabrics     using 2 fabrics

**Fig 6**

**5** From each band of strips cut off four pieces, each 1¼in (3.2cm) wide (Fig 7). Take one piece from the first band and one piece from the second. Turn the second piece through 180° (Fig 8) and place the two pieces right sides facing, matching the centre seam. Pin and stitch the two pieces together (Fig 9).

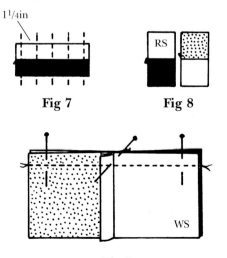

1¼in

RS

WS

**Fig 7**     **Fig 8**

**Fig 9**

Repeat this with all four pairs, making sure that each pair is pinned in *exactly* the same arrangement as the others, or your four-patches will not finish up the same (Fig 10). Press each four-patch.

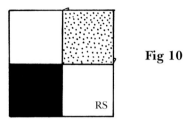

RS

**Fig 10**

**6** Place one four-patch right side *up* in the centre of the unmarked side of the foundation (Fig 11a). Hold it in position and turn the foundation over. Adjust the position of the four-patch so that the seamlines are lying exactly underneath the drawn four-patch on the foundation and the centres are matched. Pin in position. If you cannot see too well through the foundation, hold it up against the light on the sewing machine. The fabric four-patch should show beyond the marked lines by about ¼in (6mm) on all sides (Fig 11b). It helps me to think of the foundation as the curtain on the stage of a theatre: the marked side is the back of the stage curtain, to see the front of the stage you have to go round to the other side. The fabric you lay on to the other side should also face outwards towards the audience with its back to the foundation.

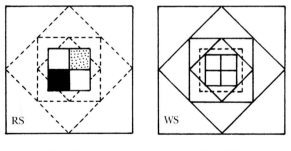

RS     WS

**Fig 11a**     **Fig 11b**

**7** Do not stitch anything at this stage. Look at your pinned four-patch and take the smallest triangle cut from the background fabric. Place it in position right side facing *outwards* on the unmarked side of the foundation – never mind the raw edges (Fig 12, page 97). The long bias edge should be next to the four-patch. Flip the triangle over on to the four-patch with right sides facing and the edges matching (Fig 13). Pin the triangle in position and turn the whole thing over so that the marked side of the foundation is uppermost.

## MAVIS HALL

*'I wanted to make an heirloom quilt for my granddaughter. Her
favourite colour is yellow so I chose the brightest shades I could find to
reflect her sunny disposition. I also personalised five extra blocks
to make it really special for her.'*

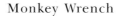

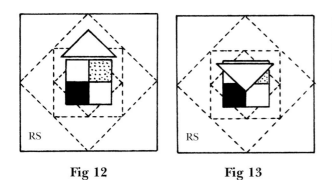

**Fig 12**　　　　　　　　**Fig 13**

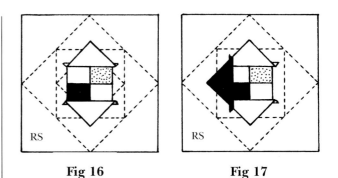

**Fig 16**　　　　　　　　**Fig 17**

**8** Stitch along the marked seamline between pieces 1 and 2, extending two or three stitches beyond the beginning and the end of the drawn line (Fig 14).

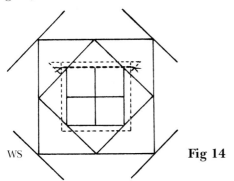

**Fig 14**

Turn to the right side and trim the seam allowance down to a scant 1/4in (6mm) by eye with a pair of sharp scissors. Flip the triangle over on to the foundation, finger press the seam and press from the front with an iron (Fig 15).

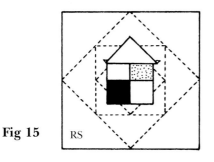

**Fig 15**

**9** Repeat this process for piece 3, marked on the foundation on the opposite side of the four-patch, using the smallest triangle of background fabric as before. Stitch along the seam between pieces 1 and 3. Press over onto the foundation as before (Fig 16).
**10** Add the triangle for the piece marked 4 on the foundation in the fabric to match the bottom left-hand square of the four-patch seen from the front of the work. Use the smallest triangle (Fig 17).

Add the triangle for piece 5 in the fabric to match the top right-hand square of the four-patch seen from the front of the work. Use the smallest triangle. Press each triangle over on to the foundation after stitching and trimming the seam. This completes Round One of the block (Fig 18).

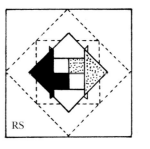

**Fig 18**

**11** Round Two is four more triangles, slightly larger and stitched on in the same way as the first set. The colours are spiralling clockwise, so check with the diagram in Fig 19 as you first lay a triangle in position right side facing *outwards* on the unmarked side of the foundation to make sure that the colour is correct. Then flip the triangle over on to the block fabric with right sides facing and the long edges matching.

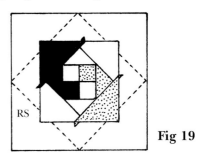

**Fig 19**

Pin or hold the piece in place and turn everything over to the marked side of the foundation. Stitch the seam and trim the seam allowance to a scant 1/4in (6mm). Flip the triangle over on to the foundation and press it in place.

**12** Round Three repeats the sequence with the next size of triangles. Round Four makes the final four corners of the block (Fig 20). Continue to add the triangles, following the sequence of numbers marked on the foundation piece with the largest triangles on the last corners. Press the completed block from the front of the work. Do not trim any of the outer edges at this stage.

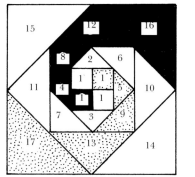

**Fig 20**

**13** Make the other three Monkey Wrench blocks in the same way as the first, using the marked foundation squares and the four-patches and triangles in exactly the same arrangement. Always check that the spirals of colour are moving clockwise as you go along. It is amazingly easy to get careless as you work on block four and think that you can remember which way the spirals go and find you have a beautifully executed but incorrect spiral on the final block. . . Press the blocks from the front.

**14** Take each block in turn and place it foundation side *up* on the cutting board. Using a rotary cutter and ruler, trim the edges to an exact ¹/4in (6mm) beyond the drawn block (Fig 21).

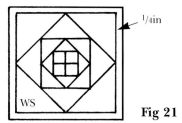

¹/4in

WS

**Fig 21**

**15** Arrange the four blocks in any way that you think most effective. Then take the top two blocks and place them right sides together. Match the drawn lines that mark the edges of the block on the foundation by pushing pins through each marked corner, in the same way as American Pieced patchwork lines are matched. Take extra care to match the points in the design that are

found at the centre of the two sides being joined (Fig 22). Stitch along the marked lines on the foundation, stitching beyond the lines right from one side of the squares to the other (Fig 23). Press the seam from the front in the opposite direction to the first pair.

Take the two bottom blocks and stitch them together in the same way as the top pair.

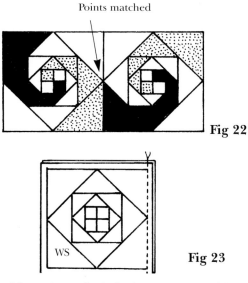

Points matched

**Fig 22**

WS

**Fig 23**

Now pin and stitch the two sets of blocks together, matching seams carefully and stitching along the marked lines on the foundations. Press the final long seam to one side, or open it if it makes the design look more balanced.

**16** It is a good idea to add the framing strips to the block while the foundation is still in place as it adds stability and the stitching line is marked ready for use. Cut framing strips, two measuring 1¹/4 x 12¹/2in (3.2 x 31.7cm) and two measuring 1¹/4 x 14in (3.2 x 35.6cm). Pin and stitch the two shorter strips to the sides of the block, stitching along the drawn line on the foundation. Press the seams outwards away from the block, pressing from the front of the work. Pin and stitch the two longer strips to the top and bottom of the block in the same way. Press seams outwards from the front of the block.

**17** Turn the block to the back and carefully remove all the paper foundation. Finally, add the sashing strips to the block (see page 130 for instructions).

## HAND OR MACHINE PIECING

# CORNER-TO-CORNER CURVE

The traditional curved block is the Drunkard's Path which is based on a square divided into two curved pieces, one of which is a quarter circle or quadrant with a radius of about two-thirds the size of the square (Fig 2, page 100). Around 1980 a softer and more subtle curved design was introduced by an American quilter Joyce Schotzhauer which became known as the Curved Two-Patch (Fig 3). The curve was not a quarter-circle but a gentler curve and ran from corner to corner across

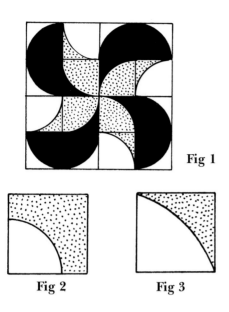

**Fig 1**

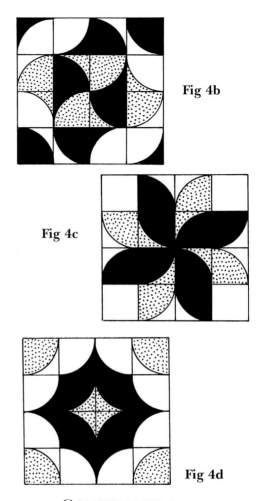

**Fig 4b**

**Fig 4c**

**Fig 2**          **Fig 3**

the square. This block was repeated and combined to make non-traditional designs often of flowers and leaves which flowed across the quilt. For the block in this New Sampler Quilt I have used the deeper quarter-circle curve which I find more effective in this restricted area, though it still runs from corner to corner of the square.

## COLOUR CHOICES

One design for the block is shown in Fig 1 and four more in Figs 4a, b, c and d. Like the traditional Drunkard's Path, all the designs are based on sixteen squares, four in each row. All use three fabrics, one of which can be a background fabric. The completed block has a finished measurement of 12 x 12in (30.5 x 30.5cm), and an inner frame of ³/₄in (1.9cm) finished width will be needed around the block before the sashing strips, so this extra colour should be considered when choices are being made. Study your chosen design and decide which fabric is to go where. You may find it easier to make a rough sketch or tracing of the block and colour it so that you can count how many of each shape you need to cut from each fabric.

**Fig 4d**

## CONSTRUCTION

1 Templates for the two shapes in the design are given in Fig 5. The outer solid line is the cutting line and *includes* the ¹/₄in (6mm) seam allowance. If you want to stitch the block by machine, make card or plastic templates by tracing in the usual way, marking the directional arrows but ignoring the dotted stitching lines shown on each template.

If you want to hand-stitch in the American Piecing method, you should make templates without the seam allowances, but this presents a problem as the sharp corners on the dotted inner lines on piece B taper away to such a long, fine point that it is almost impossible to make a template from it and to draw round it accurately. One solution is to make the templates with the seam allowances added and just judge the ¹/₄in (6mm) seam allowance by eye as you stitch. If this is not easy for you to do accurately (I find it really hard), then make the same templates as for machine piecing. Mark on them only the *curved* dotted stitching lines and the directional arrows (Fig 6). Do *not* cut along the dotted lines. Draw the curved

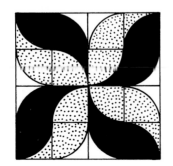

**Fig 4a**

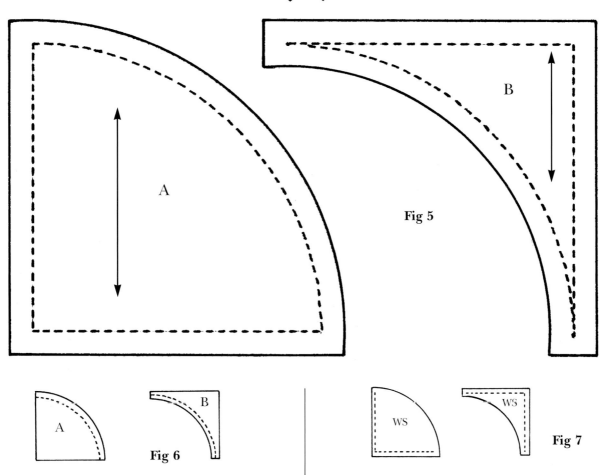

**Fig 5**

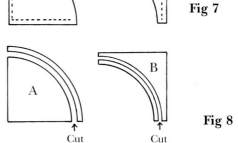

**Fig 6**

**Fig 7**

**Fig 8**

Cut          Cut

dotted lines on the template and then ignore them for the moment. They will be used later when adding stitching lines.

**2** Whichever way you intend to stitch the block, the first drawing and cutting stage is the same. On the wrong side of each chosen fabric draw accurately around the templates using a sharp marking pencil and matching the direction of the arrows with the weave or grain of the fabric. Unlike American Piecing, the drawn line is the *cutting* line, so you do not have to allow extra space for seam allowances. Just position the drawn shapes as close as possible to save fabric.

**3** Cut out each drawn shape exactly on the drawn line. A rotary cutter and ruler can be used for the straight edges if preferred, but a pair of scissors is probably best for the curved edges.

**4** If you are a hand-stitcher and need to mark the stitching line, a ruler and sharp marking pencil can be used for the straight sides to mark the ¹/₄in (6mm) seam allowance. Mark these lines on the *wrong* side of each cut fabric shape (Fig 7). To mark the stitching line on the curved edge, first trim each template along the dotted stitching line marked on its *curved* edge only (Fig 8). Only do this once you have cut out all the shapes for the

design using the complete templates from Fig 5.

Place the trimmed template A on to the *wrong* side of one of the cut quarter-circles of fabric, lining up the two straight edges on the template with the cut straight edges of the fabric (Fig 9). Draw along the curved edge of the template to make the curved stitching line on the fabric (Fig 10).

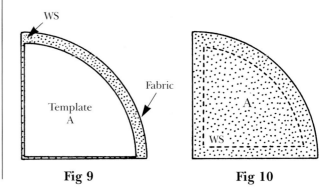

**Fig 9**          **Fig 10**

## SHIRLEY PRESCOTT

*'Having accumulated quite a lot of fabrics over the years, I decided to try to make this quilt without buying any more. In the end I had to buy one half metre of red chintz for the border.*
*As machine piecing is my preference, the hand-sewn blocks were a real challenge. I must admit to being very happy with the final result.'*

Mark the curved stitching line on each cut quarter-circle shape of the design in the same way. Use the trimmed template B to mark the curved stitching line on all the smaller cut shapes (Fig 11).

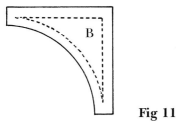

**Fig 11**

**5** Arrange the cut pieces in your chosen design on a flat surface or pin them in position on a polystyrene tile or board. Changes can be made at this stage before any stitching is done.

**6** Take the two shapes A and B which make up one of the sixteen squares in the design and fold each one in half along its curved edge, pinching it firmly to mark the centre of the curve with a crease. Do *not* clip any curved edges. With right sides *facing* and the smaller piece B on top, match the centre creases. The edges of both fabrics should be level with each other. Pin as shown in Fig 12.

**7** Swing each corner of shape B round and pin in position at the corners of shape A, lining up the edges of both fabrics (Fig 13). If the seam is to be machined, no more pins are necessary.

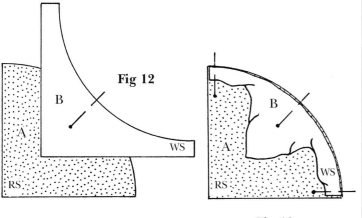

**Fig 12**

**Fig 13**

**8** Place the pinned fabrics with the smaller piece B uppermost on the machine and stitch an exact ¼in (6mm) seam from pinned corner to pinned corner. The trick is to use the point of a stitch-ripper or a long pin to pull the two edges into alignment no more than ½in (1.2cm) ahead of the needle as you stitch. The top fabric will

stretch easily, as the curve is cut on the bias. It will probably take a couple of tries to get a perfect result, but once you are used to stretching the fabric a little at a time, the resulting curves are accurate and very quickly achieved. The stitched ¼in (6mm) seam should begin and finish midway on the narrow ends of shape B to keep the completed square an accurate shape (Fig 14).

**9** If stitching by hand, add more pins to the original three if you wish, stretching the top fabric shape B over your hand to ease it to fit against shape A. Line up the edges of the fabric and begin to stitch from the marked corner of the design, following the drawn stitching line on the top fabric shape B. Check that your stitches are also running through the marked line drawn on the underneath fabric shape A. If the two edges of the fabrics are always exactly matched, this should not be a problem. Stitch with small running stitches and the occasional backstitch in the American hand-piecing technique.

**10** Once all sixteen seams are stitched, press the squares from the front with the seams pressed towards the smaller shape B (Fig 15). Arrange the squares in your chosen design.

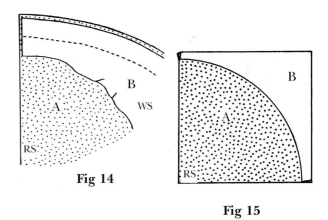

**Fig 14**

**Fig 15**

**11** Join the squares into horizontal rows, pinning and matching the seams and stitching either by hand or by machine. If stitching by machine, press the seams from the front, ironing the seams of row one in one direction, those in row two the opposite way and so on. Join the rows together, matching the seams carefully. Press the completed block from the front of the work.

**12** The block should measure 12½ x 12½in (31.7 x 31.7cm). Add the inner framing strips of a cut width of 1¼in (3.2cm) to bring the block up to 14 x 14in (35.6 x 35.6cm). Finally, add the sashing strips (see page 130 for instructions).

# MARINER'S COMPASS

**M**ariner's Compass is a traditional pieced patchwork block which many quilters find daunting because of the exact piecing necessary to achieve such fine points. It is now made painless and accurate through foundation piecing on freezer paper and a sixteen-point compass is included in this Sampler Quilt (Fig 1). Once you have made this, it is possible to piece other larger or more complex compasses. Hand-workers can use the technique easily to piece the block by hand.

**Fig 1**

## COLOUR CHOICES

Two fabrics are used for the points of the compass, one for the longer set of points which alternates with the shorter set made from the second fabric. The compass is set into a circular background and then placed within another background fabric to make the square block. These two background areas can be of the same fabric, so that the compass floats in the block, or of two different fabrics. Towards the centre of the block are small triangular pieces which look best in a contrasting fabric to the main compass. The centre circle is added last of all, so it is probably best to leave that choice of fabric until the rest of the block is assembled when it is easier to judge what looks best.

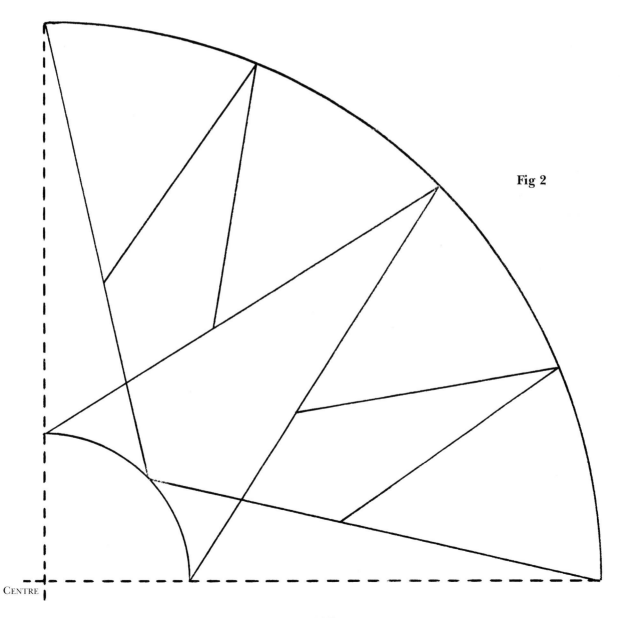

**Fig 2**

Centre

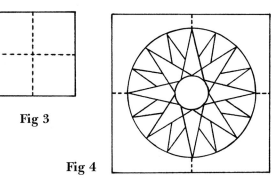

**Fig 3**

**Fig 4**

## CONSTRUCTION

**1** Fig 2 shows one quarter of the compass design. Take a square of freezer paper measuring 13 x 13in (33 x 33cm) and fold the paper into four quarters (Fig 3). Unfold it and trace the quarter compass from Fig 2 four times on the freezer paper using the folded lines on the paper as a guide to positioning each section (Fig 4). Number each piece in the order shown in Fig 5.

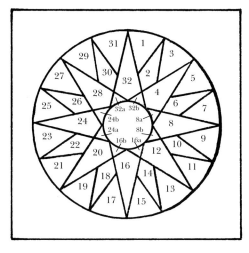

**Fig 5**

**2** From the fabric chosen for the final background square (not the inner background to the compass), cut a square 13½ x 13½in (34.3 x 34.3cm). Press lightly with an iron into four quarters. Cut out the circular design from the freezer paper in one piece but do not start cutting it up into little pieces yet!

**3** Place the circle of freezer paper shiny side *down* on to the *wrong* side of the square of background fabric using the fold lines in the fabric to help position the circle exactly in the centre. Press with an iron (wool setting, no steam) to stick the freezer paper on to the fabric. Draw round the paper circle with a fabric-marking pencil, also marking where the compass points touch the edge of the

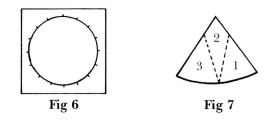

**Fig 6**

**Fig 7**

circle. Remove the paper circle (Fig 6). This fabric square will not be needed until the compass is completed.

**4** From the paper compass cut out the wedge shape made from pieces 1–2–3 (Fig 7). In the same way cut out the seven similar wedge shapes (pieces 5–6–7, 9–10–11, 13–14–15, 17–18–19, 21–22–23, 25–26–27, 29–30–31), leaving the longer points still joined to the centre.

### *Piecing the Wedge Sections*

**5** It is easier here to use templates for the fabric that is to be cut and pieced onto the freezer paper. Make card templates by tracing shapes A and B from Fig 8 or use template plastic, marking the grain-line arrows. Shape A has been drawn to include an exact ¼in (6mm) seam allowance, while shape B includes a more generous seam allowance of ½in (1.2cm) as this makes it easier to piece.

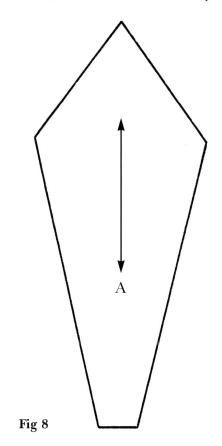

A

**Fig 8**

**Fig 8**

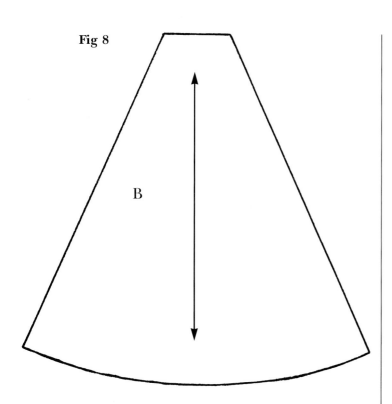

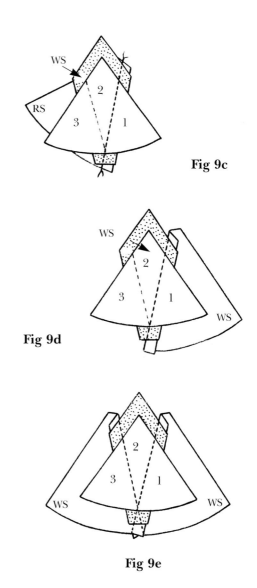

Fig 9c

Fig 9d

Fig 9e

**6** From template A cut eight shapes from the fabric chosen for the smaller compass points. No extra seam allowance is needed, so the cutting can be done more quickly by folding the fabric into four layers, drawing round the template on the top layer and cutting several shapes at once with a rotary cutter. In the same way use template B to cut sixteen shapes from the inner background fabric.

**7** Take the freezer paper wedge with 1–2–3 written on it. Place it shiny side *down* with the central area on the *wrong* side of a cut piece of fabric from template A (Fig 9a). Use an iron to press the paper on to the fabric. Pin a cut piece of fabric from template B (the inner background fabric) right sides together with fabric A, matching the long edges. Make sure the curved edge is positioned as in Fig 9b.

Turn the paper over and stitch along the drawn line (Fig 9c). Press fabric B out on to the freezer paper (Fig 9d). Take a second cut piece of fabric B and repeat the process on the remaining section of the paper wedge (Fig 9e). Trim the fabric edges down to ¼in (6mm) on all sides, using a ruler for the straight edges and trimming the bottom curve by eye (Fig 10).

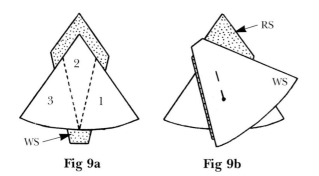

**Fig 9a**      **Fig 9b**

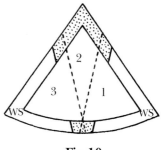

**Fig 10**

MARY HARROWELL

*'The choice of fabrics reflects my love of flowers and I call it my Garden Flowers Quilt. The blocks were joined together before backing with calico and then quilted as a whole piece, making it reversible.'*

**8** From the freezer paper compass, cut points 4, 12, 20 and 28. Press these shiny side *down* onto the *back* of the fabric chosen for the longer points, leaving at least ½in (1.2cm) between each shape and placing them so that the grain of the fabric lies along the centre of each shape (Fig 11).

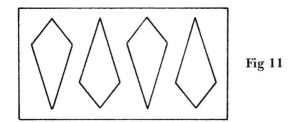

**Fig 11**

Cut out each piece with a ¼in (6mm) seam allowance on all sides, using a rotary cutter and ruler for accuracy (Fig 12). The edge of the paper marks the stitching line. It is useful to draw lines with a sharp marking pencil at the corners of each shape. This marks the exact corners in case the freezer paper peels back while being handled (Fig 13).

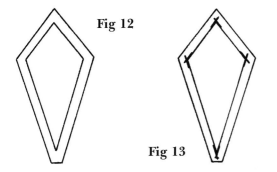

**Fig 12**

**Fig 13**

**9** Cut the remaining four points 8, 16, 24 and 32 from the centre circle, including with them the small triangular shapes a and b (Fig 14). Iron each paper shape onto the back of the chosen fabric, leaving at least ½in (1.2cm) between each shape.

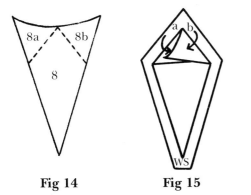

**Fig 14**

**Fig 15**

Pull back each of the a and b points and fold them back on the drawn line. Now cut around the paper shapes adding a ¼in (6mm) seam allowance (Fig 15).

**10** From the fabric chosen for the a and b triangles cut eight squares, each measuring 1½ x 1½in (3.9 x 3.9cm). Take piece number 8, unfold the paper points a and b and iron them down onto the fabric as before. Turn the piece over so that the fabric side is uppermost. Place a fabric square right side *down* onto piece 8, matching edges as in Fig 16. Hold it in position while you turn everything over. Stitch along the drawn line (Fig 17). Press the square of fabric out onto the freezer paper (Fig 18).

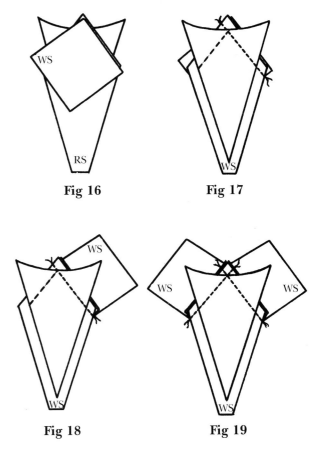

**Fig 16**          **Fig 17**

**Fig 18**          **Fig 19**

**11** In the same way stitch a second square to the other side of piece 8. Press the square out onto the freezer paper (Fig 19). Trim squares a and b to match the paper shape, adding a ¼in (6mm) seam allowance (Fig 20). Repeat this process with pieces 16, 24 and 32.

**12** Mark the corners of the freezer paper on the fabric in case the paper lifts off when handled. If it does come loose, iron it down again.

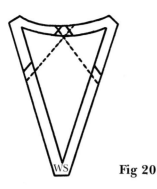

**Fig 20**

### Assembling the Compass

**13** Arrange the compass design, paper sides uppermost with the numbered pieces lying consecutively as in the original plan. Pin wedge 1–2–3 and piece 4 together with right sides facing. Match the corners of the freezer paper with a pin at either end of the seam and line up the edges of the fabric. Sew along the edges of the freezer paper including the seam allowance at either end (Fig 21). Press the seam towards the wedge shape. If any freezer paper has been caught in the underneath seam, ease it out carefully. If it is caught really badly, unpick that small section and re-stitch it.

Pin and stitch wedge 5–6–7 to the compass and then the long point 8–8a–8b, matching corners and intersecting seams carefully and pressing seams away from the long points each time (Fig 22).

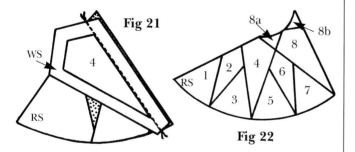

**Fig 21**

**Fig 22**

Piece the compass in four sections (Fig 23) and finally join the sections together. Mark the outer curved stitching line by drawing along the curved edge of the freezer paper, then remove all the paper from the block.

### Adding the Centre Circle

**14** Iron the freezer paper circle (the remaining piece) to the *back* of the fabric chosen for the centre. Cut out the fabric with a 1/4in (6mm) seam allowance. Peel the freezer paper from the fabric and reverse it, pinning it onto the *back* of the fabric circle with shiny side *upwards* (Fig 24). Use the nose of the iron to nudge the seam allowance

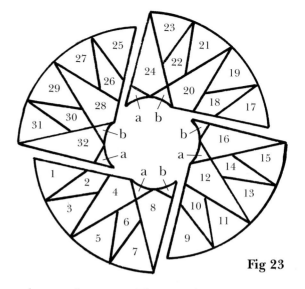

**Fig 23**

evenly over the paper (Fig 25). Pin the centre in position on the assembled compass with the grain of the circle horizontal to the compass and appliqué it into place. Remove the freezer paper from the back after stitching.

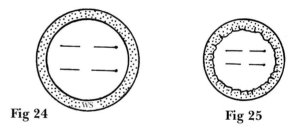

**Fig 24**

**Fig 25**

### Attaching the Outer Background Section

**15** Take the marked square of background fabric (prepared previously in steps 2 and 3) and cut away the centre part, leaving a 1/4in (6mm) seam allowance in the inner section. Clip the curve to within 1/8in (3mm) of the drawn line (Fig 26). With right sides facing, pin the background circle to the compass, matching the marks on the drawn circle with the points on the compass. Check that the compass is positioned with the north-south axis vertical in the background square before stitching along the marked seamline to set the compass in its background frame. Press the block from the front with the final seam pressed towards the outer frame.

**16** Add the inner framing strips to bring the block up to exactly 14 x 14in (35.6 x 35.6cm), then add the sashing strips. See page 130 for framing and sashing.

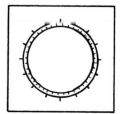

**Fig 26**

Hand Stitching

# Celtic Appliqué

The design used in the block of Celtic Knot patchwork in this New Sampler Quilt was made by outlining the fabric pieces with ¼in (6mm) bias strips. Similar bias strips were used in the Carolina Lily block for the curvy stems. In this block an appliqué design of a lily is outlined with narrow bias strips ⅛in (3mm) wide (Fig 1), a technique originated by Philomena Durcan, the leading exponent of Celtic patchwork.

This technique does not follow the Celtic

**Fig 1**

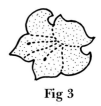

**Fig 3**

principle of bias strips weaving over and under each other. Instead the fabric pieces of the lily and leaves are tacked in position on to a background and then outlined with the bias strips, which are laid on in sequence so that the raw ends of one strip are covered by another strip positioned later in the sequence. The edges of the appliqué do not have to be neatened as they are covered by the bias strips. Working out the order of pinning and stitching the bias strips is the key to this technique, just as it is with traditional hand appliqué blocks.

## COLOUR CHOICES

The lily design is set on a background fabric, so if you are using one fabric throughout as a background on your quilt you will need it here. The lily is cut from one piece of fabric and the four leaves from another. Realism does not have to play a part here: your flower and leaves can be from any shades that you are using in your quilt. The outlining narrow bias strips can be made from two fabrics – one to outline the petals of the flower, and another around the leaves and for the stems and tendrils. Alternatively, one fabric can be used throughout for all the edgings to keep the design simpler.

## CONSTRUCTION

**1** Cut a square of fabric for the background measuring 12$\frac{1}{2}$ x 12$\frac{1}{2}$in (31.7 x 31.7cm).
**2** Mark the lily and leaf design from the two sections of Fig 2 (on pages 114 and 115) very lightly on the *right* side of the background fabric, using a sharp marking pencil and a light box if necessary. If the fabric is too dark for the design to be traced through, use dressmaker's carbon paper and a tracing wheel. (I use an empty fine ballpoint pen to mark the design through the carbon paper.)
**3** In the same way trace the lily flower on to the *right* side of the chosen lily fabric. Match the grain or weave of the lily fabric with the arrows marked on the lily in Fig 2. Cut the drawn flower shape

out around its outer edge (see Fig 3). Place it in position over the drawn lily shape on the background fabric, then pin and tack the lily in place.
**4** In the same way, trace each of the four leaves on to the *front* of the chosen fabric. Match the grain of the fabric with the arrows on the leaf shapes in Fig 2. Cut out each leaf and pin in position over the drawn outlines on the background fabric. Tack each leaf in place.

### Making the Bias Tubing

**5** The bias strips needed to make the narrow $\frac{1}{8}$in (3mm) wide bias edging can all be cut from a 12in (30.5cm) square of fabric, assuming you are going to use one fabric throughout. If you want to use several different fabrics, cut and stitch the bias tubes from each fabric as you need them.

The bias strips must be cut $\frac{3}{4}$in (1.9cm) in width. First cut the 12in (30.5cm) square of fabric to be used for the bias edging in half diagonally (Fig 4). Take one of the cut triangles of fabric and turn it on the cutting board so that the cut diagonal edge is to the left and move the ruler over it until the cut edge lines up with the $\frac{3}{4}$in (1.9cm) marking on the ruler (Fig 5). Cut along the right side of the ruler. (Left-handers should turn the fabric and cut from the right, not the left.) Cut seven strips from the triangle of fabric. Repeat this with the other triangle, cutting fourteen strips in total. Before folding and stitching the cut strips, use a short sample length of strip cut from the left-over fabric first to get the sizing right.

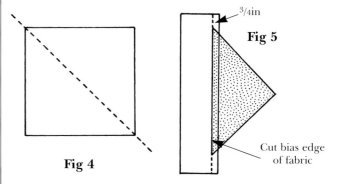

**Fig 4**

**Fig 5**

$\frac{3}{4}$in

Cut bias edge of fabric

**6** Take the strip and fold in half lengthways with the right side *outside*. Don't pull the strip to make the edges match or it will stretch and become narrower. Using a smaller stitch than usual, machine-stitch a seam by eye *midway* down the folded strip (Fig 6, page 115). This makes a tube that is a generous $\frac{1}{8}$in (3mm) in width, which you

## PAM CROGER

*'Having been lucky enough to buy fabric on holiday in America, I thought I was well away.
But why didn't I buy enough to start with, instead of having to persuade long-suffering friends
to shop for me on their trips to the States!'*

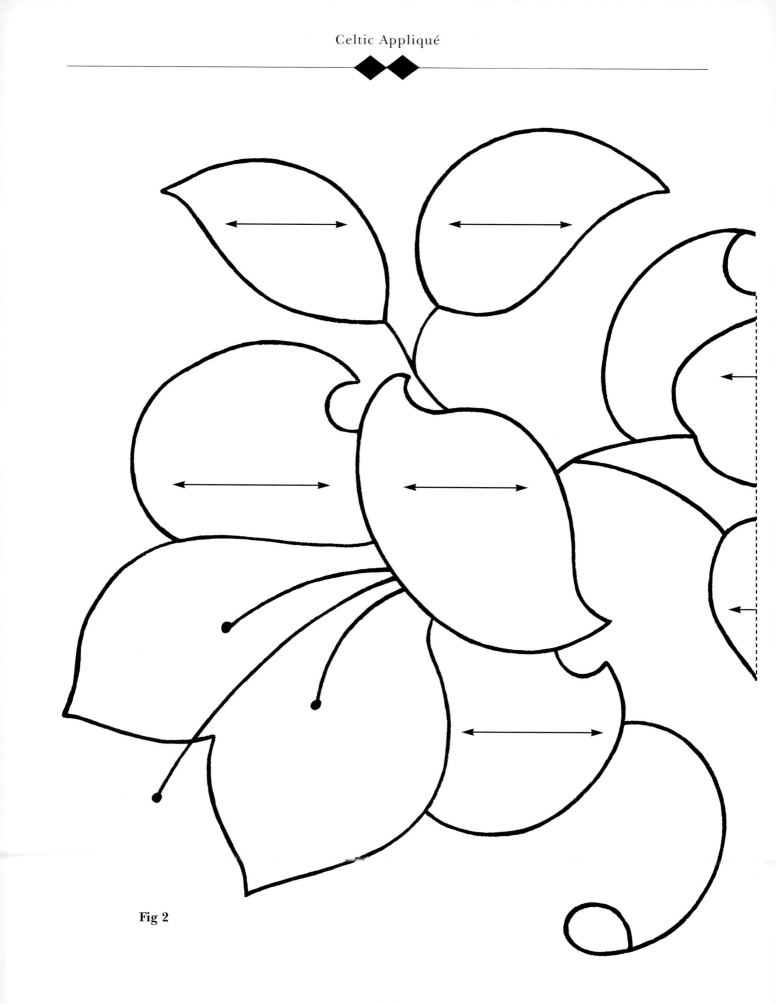

**Fig 2**

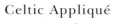

will find much easier to slide the bias bar through. Check that the bar will just slip into the tube – it needs to fit snugly without any slack (Fig 7a).

**7** Trim the seams very close to the stitching without cutting the stitches. Slide the bar into the tube, twisting the fabric so that both seam and seam allowance lie across one flat side of the bar and cannot be seen from the other side (Fig 7b). With the bar in place, press the seam allowance to one side, using a steam iron for added firmness.

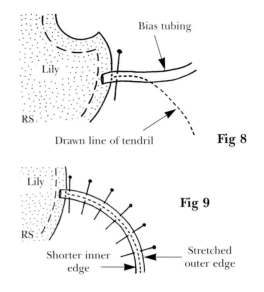

**Fig 8**

**Fig 9**

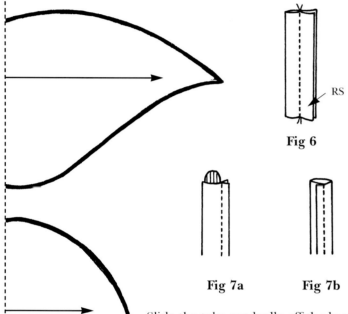

**Fig 6**

**Fig 7a** **Fig 7b**

Slide the tube gradually off the bar, pressing firmly as you go. Stitch and press all the cut bias strips in this way.

**8** Begin by pinning and stitching the lower curly tendril as this has no angled turns to manage. Take a short length of pressed bias tubing about 7in (17.8cm) long and trim one end at right angles to the tube. Pin this end onto the background fabric over the drawn line of the tendril where it meets the lily petal. The drawn line should lie midway underneath the bias tube. Leave the raw end of the tube extending 1/8in (3mm) beyond the start of the tendril so that it can be hidden under the bias stem later (Fig 8). Pin the bias tube over the drawn line of the tendril, positioning the shorter inside edge first and stretching it slightly on the curves so that there are no tiny puckers along that edge. The longer outside edge has to stretch a little more to fit the curve but as it is cut on the bias this is not a problem (Fig 9).

Pin about every 1/2in (1.2cm) at right angles to the bias tubing. You could pin the entire tendril in place before stitching or just pin a short distance ahead of the stitching as you work. Always stitch the shorter inside edge first. You probably won't need any pins to hold the outer edge in position once the inside edge has been stitched in place. The curled end of the tendril needs to be stretched around and pinned so that its raw end is trapped underneath the pinned tendril (Fig 10). This end is held in place when the tendril is stitched over it.

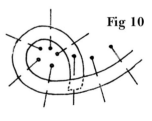

**Fig 10**

**9** Pin and stitch the other tendril in the same way, leaving an extra 1/8in (3mm) where it meets the stem of the adjacent leaf.

**10** Each of the two pairs of leaves has the right-hand leaf joining the main stem of the left-hand leaf. Edge the right-hand leaf first. Take a piece of pressed bias tube about 12in (30.5cm) in length. Pin and stitch it in position around the leaf with the inner edge lying on the leaf itself and the outer edge *just* on the background fabric. This means that nearly all the pressed tube is positioned over the leaf and when stitched in place secures the raw edge of the leaf safely under it (Fig 11, page 116).

Pin and stitch the bias tube in the direction shown in Fig 12, stitching the shorter inner edges first. Leave an extra 1/8in (3mm) beyond the starting point so that it can be covered later by the bias tubing on the other side of the leaf. Turning the sharp corner at the top of the leaf is not as

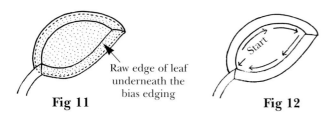

**Fig 11** Raw edge of leaf underneath the bias edging

**Fig 12** Start

difficult as it looks. Pin and stitch the inner edge of the bias tube to within 1/4in (6mm) of the turning point. Use a large pin to catch the outer edge of the tube at its turning point. Pin this into the fabric as shown in Fig 13. Pull the bias tube sharply round so that it lies in position on the edge of the leaf, tucking under the fold of fabric at the sharp corner with the needle until it makes a mitre. Pull back the large pin and reposition the point to hold the mitred fold in place (Fig 14).

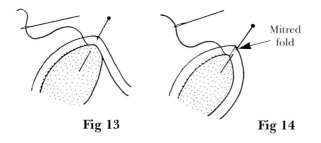

**Fig 13**

**Fig 14** Mitred fold

Continue to pin and stitch the bias tube onto the second side of the leaf. Do not stitch the mitre itself (Fig 15). At the base of the leaf, twist the bias tube to cover the raw end of the stitched tube, using a pin as before to mitre the angle and continue with the tube to pin and stitch the stem (Fig 16). Once the inner edges are stitched, sew the outer edges of the tube in place. Leave an extra 1/8in (3mm) of tubing where it joins the main stem – this will eventually be covered by the main stem.

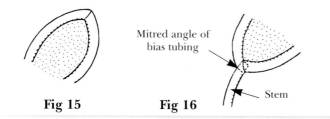

**Fig 15** **Fig 16** Mitred angle of bias tubing / Stem

**11** Cut a piece of bias tubing about 12in (30.5cm) in length and pin and stitch it around the second leaf in the same way. Its stem should cover the raw edges of the side stems and finish at the lily petal. Trim the end to 1/8in (3mm) beyond the edge of the petal. This end will eventually be covered by the bias edging around the petal itself.

**12** Edge the other pair of leaves in the same way.
**13** Pin and stitch a 7in (17.8cm) length of bias tubing around each of the two side petals marked 1 and 2 in Fig 17, mitring the sharp corners and leaving an extra 1/8in (3mm) at either end as before.
**14** Pin and stitch a length of bias tubing about 12in (30.5cm) long around the centre petal marked 3 in Fig 17, covering the raw ends of side petals 1 and 2. Leave an extra 1/8in (3mm) at either end as before.

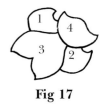

**Fig 17**

**15** The three stamens are made from three lengths of bias tubing, one about 5in (12.7cm) long and the other two about 3in (7.6cm) long. The stamen end is made by tying a knot in the tubing about 1/2in (1.2cm) from one end (Fig 18a). Bring the end across the knot (Fig 18b) and tuck it behind the knot (Fig 18c). Secure the end to the back of the knot with a few stitches. The knotted stamen can then be pinned in position, pinning from the knotted end and trimming the other end to leave an extra 1/8in (3mm) where the stamen meets the petal. Stitch the stamen – inner curve first. Knot and stitch all three stamens in this way.

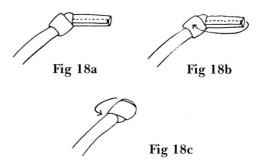

**Fig 18a** **Fig 18b**

**Fig 18c**

**16** Finally, pin and stitch petal 4 (Fig 17), beginning at a sharp corner so that the raw ends can be tucked under without it being too obvious.
**17** Trim the completed block to an exact 12 x 12in (30.5 x 30.5cm) square. Cut two strips for the inner frame each measuring 1 1/2 x 12in (3.9 x 30.5cm) and two measuring 1 1/2 x 14in (3.9 x 35.6cm). Pin and stitch the two shorter strips to the either side of the block. Press the seams outwards away from the block, pressing from the front of the work. Pin and stitch the two longer strips to the top and bottom of the block. Press seams outwards, pressing from the front as before. Finally, add the sashing strips to the block (see page 130 for instructions).

## MACHINE FOUNDATION PIECING

# ELECTRIC FAN

This block has an Art Deco feel to it (see Fig 1) and fits in well with the other blocks in this New Sampler Quilt. Four pieced rectangles are arranged around a centre square with the centre circle appliquéd onto the block once piecing is completed

(Fig 2). The circle can be omitted if preferred. Each of the four rectangles is made up of two larger curved shapes with a pieced curved strip between them. If this section is pieced on a foundation, the block can be assembled without too much heartache.

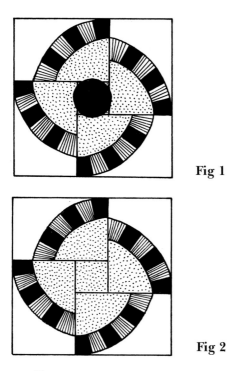

**Fig 1**

**Fig 2**

## COLOUR CHOICES

The Electric Fan is set on a background fabric in the four corners of the block. The main central part of the fan is made from one fabric, with another two fabrics used alternately to form the pieced outer edge of the fan. A completely different fabric can be chosen for the centre circle or one already used in the pieced fan edge. I am inclined to leave that decision until the rest of the block has been assembled.

## CONSTRUCTION

**1** Make card templates of shapes A and B from Fig 3 (page 119) by tracing them, cutting them out and sticking them on to card, or use template plastic. Mark the directional arrows, as these show how the template should be positioned on the grain or weave of the fabric. The stitching line is shown as a dotted line within the templates. Mark the templates so that you know which way up to use them, as they are *not* reversible.

**2** Shape C *only* is to be pieced using the foundation-piecing method. Choose a foundation that can be removed once the piecing is complete, such as tracing paper, freezer paper or a woven tear-away foundation. Trace shape C four times on to your chosen foundation, tracing all the drawn lines and numbers (Fig 4). No space needs to

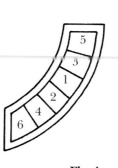

**Fig 4**

be left between each drawn shape. Cut round each shape C, cutting exactly on the outer drawn line.

**3** On the *wrong* side of the fabric chosen for the central area of the block, draw round template A four times. Check that this template is used *right side up*. Do not flip it over, or the design will not fit together properly. Match the grain of the fabric with the directional arrow drawn on the template. Cut out each shape exactly on the drawn line (seam allowances are included in the template). In addition, from this fabric cut a square measuring 3 x 3in (7.6 x 7.6cm) for the square that will be pieced into the centre of the block.

**4** On the *wrong* side of the background fabric to be used in the corners of the block draw round template B four times. Match the grain of the fabric to the drawn arrow on the template. Cut out the four shapes exactly on the drawn line. Use the template *right side up* – do not flip it over or the design will not fit together.

### *Foundation Piecing the Curved Strip*

**5** From each of the two fabrics to be used, cut a strip measuring 2½ x 26in (6.3 x 66cm) (two shorter lengths will be fine if you haven't got a 26in (66cm) length in the chosen fabric).

From each strip cut eight pieces 2in (5cm) wide and four pieces 2½in (6.3cm) wide. You should finish up with two sets of pieces as shown in Fig 5. The larger pieces are to be used for the *end* sections on each strip as they are bigger than the middle four pieces.

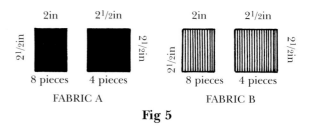

**Fig 5**

**6** Follow the general instructions for foundation piecing given on page 93 to set your machine up ready for stitching. Place a rectangle of one of the chosen fabrics 2½ x 2in (6.3 x 5cm) right side *up* on the unmarked side of the foundation over the section marked 1 (Fig 6).

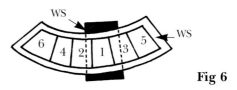

**Fig 6**

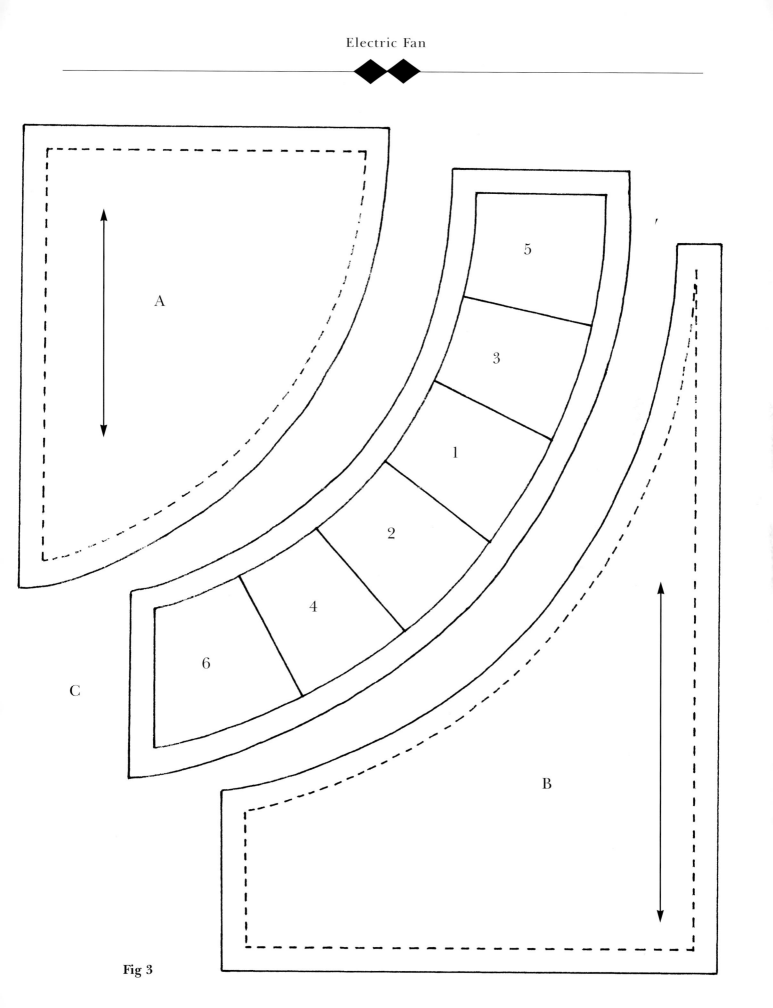

**Fig 3**

The longer side should stretch from one edge of the foundation strip to the other. Hold it in position and turn the foundation over to the marked side. Adjust the position of the fabric so that there is at least ¼in (6mm) beyond the marked lines on all sides. If you can't see too well through the foundation, hold it up against the light on the sewing machine. Pin in position.

The sections on the foundation are wedge-shaped so the amount of fabric extending beyond the drawn lines will not be a regular ¼in (6mm). I find it helpful to correct this before adding each new piece of fabric as it makes the positioning easier. To do this, fold back and crease the foundation on to the marked back along the line between sections 1 and 2 (Fig 7). I use a thin plastic 6in (15.2cm) ruler placed along the drawn line to help me. Fold back the foundation against the edge of the ruler to get an accurate crease. Trim the fabric beyond this creased edge by eye to ¼in (6mm). Unfold the foundation so that it lies flat again.

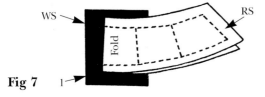

**Fig 7**

**7** Take a rectangle of the second fabric 2½ x 2in (6.3 x 5cm) and place it right side *up* in the correct position over section 2 on the unmarked side of the foundation. You can see where to position it by looking through from the marked side of the foundation. Flip the rectangle of fabric over on to the original pinned fabric with right sides facing. Line up the fabric edges at the seam to be stitched and pin if necessary (fig 8). If you would prefer just to hold the pieces in place, then do so.

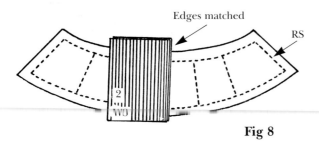

Edges matched

**Fig 8**

**8** Turn the foundation over so that the marked side is uppermost and place it on the machine. Stitch along the line between sections 1 and 2, extending right across the foundation at the beginning and end of the drawn line (Fig 9). Flip

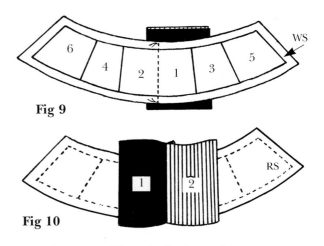

**Fig 9**

**Fig 10**

over piece 2 and iron it flat in position over section 2 on the foundation (Fig 10).

**9** Use the thin ruler to fold back and crease the foundation on to the marked back along the seam between section 1 and section 3. Trim the fabric beyond the creased edge by eye to ¼in (6mm) as before. Unfold the foundation so that it lies flat again.

**10** Place a rectangle of the second fabric 2½ x 2in (6.3 x 5cm) right side up in the correct position over section 3 on the unmarked side of the foundation. Flip the fabric rectangle over on to the original fabric piece 1, right sides facing. Line up the fabric edges at the seam to be stitched. Pin or hold the fabric in position and turn the foundation over to the marked side. Stitch along the seam between sections 1 and 3, extending right across the foundation at the beginning and end of the drawn line. Flip over piece 3 and iron it flat in position over section 3 on the foundation (Fig 11, page 122).

**11** Continue to position and stitch each piece of fabric in place on the foundation, following the numbers. Trim the existing seam allowance each time before adding the new piece of fabric by folding the foundation back on the seamline to be stitched and trimming the fabric. Alternate the

### MAUREEN BLOYS

*'Of all the blocks, Tangled Star holds special memories for me as I stitched it while on holiday. The Corner-to-Corner block is another favourite which varies greatly in layout and arrangement of fabrics from quilt to quilt.'*

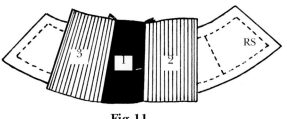

**Fig 11**

fabrics as you add each piece on the foundation. Use the larger fabric squares, 2½ x 2½in (6.3 x 6.3cm), for the end sections as these are slightly wider than the rest.

**12**  Press the completed curved strip and trim the fabric to match the *outer* edges of the foundation.

**13**  In the same way, stitch the fabric rectangles and squares on to the other three foundation strips. Make sure the colours are used in the same alternating arrangement each time. Trim the fabric edges to match the *outer* edges of the foundation.

**14**  Remove the foundation, taking care not to undo the stitches at either end of the stitched seams.

### Assembling the Block

**15**  The four rectangular sections can now be pieced, each one as shown in Fig 12. Fold the curved edge of shape A in half to find the centre. Do the same with shape C. Pin the curved edge of shape A to the shorter curved edge of shape C, matching the centres and corners. I find it easiest to pin and stitch with shape C on top. Like all curved seams, it may need quite a few pins placed at right angles to the seam. Clip the curved seam allowance of piece C if necessary to help fit the pieces together. Stitch the usual ¼in (6mm) seam. Press the seam allowance towards the pieced strip.

**16**  In the same way pin and stitch the large piece B to the pieced strip, working with piece B on the top, stretching it slightly to fit where necessary. Press the seam allowance towards piece B. Make all four rectangles in the same way.

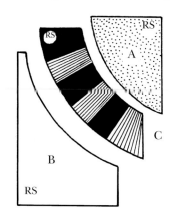

**Fig 12**

**17**  Arrange the rectangles together with the 3 x 3in (7.6 x 7.6cm) square cut for the centre of the block (Fig 13). They are assembled in the same way as the Folded Flying Geese in that block.

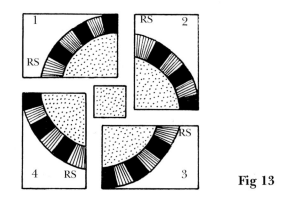

**Fig 13**

**18**  Stitch the centre square to unit 1, stitching about *halfway* along the seam only (Fig 14). Open the square out away from unit 1, pressing the seam allowance towards unit 1.

Pin and stitch unit 2 to the side of unit 1 and the centre square (Fig 15). Press the seam towards unit 2.

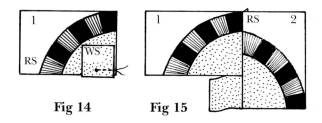

**Fig 14**          **Fig 15**

Pin and stitch unit 3 to the bottom of unit 2 and the centre square (Fig 16). Press the seam towards unit 3.

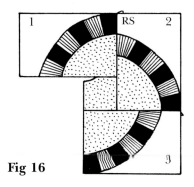

**Fig 16**

Pin and stitch unit 4 to the side of unit 3 and the centre square (Fig 17). Press the seam towards unit 4.

Finally, stitch the seam to join the top of unit 4 and the square to unit 1. Press the seam towards unit 1.

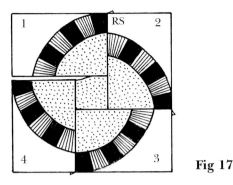

**Fig 17**

### Making the Centre Circle

**19**  Trace the circle in Fig 18 on to the non-shiny side of freezer paper, or use a pair of compasses to draw a circle with a radius of 1¹/₄in (3.2cm). Cut out the circle exactly on the drawn line.

**20**  Iron the circle shiny side *down* on to the *wrong* side of the fabric chosen for the centre circle in the block. Cut out the circle adding a ¹/₄in (6mm) seam allowance to the fabric (Fig 19).

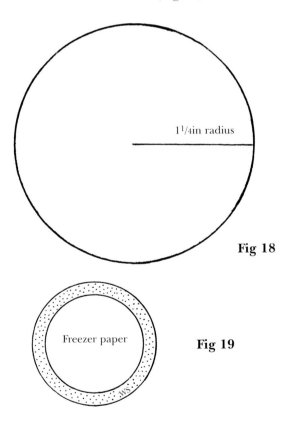

1¹/₄in radius

**Fig 18**

Freezer paper

**Fig 19**

**21**  Peel the paper circle off the fabric and replace it shiny side *up* on the *wrong* side of the fabric circle in exactly the same position, leaving the ¹/₄in (6mm) seam allowance on all sides. Pin the freezer paper on to the fabric (Fig 20). Using the side of an iron (no steam, wool setting), nudge the seam

allowance of fabric over on to the freezer paper, easing in the fullness a little at a time until all the seam allowance is stuck down on the paper. Keep the curve smooth without any tiny pleats (Fig 21).

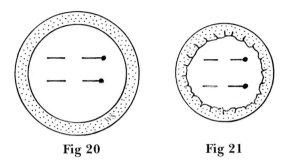

**Fig 20**          **Fig 21**

**22**  Position the fabric circle over the centre square in the block. It can be ironed on but may still need pins to stop it from shifting as you stitch it into place. Match the grain of the circle with the grain of fabric in the rest of the block. Stitch the circle by hand, using small appliqué stitches in a thread colour to match the circle, not the background.

**23**  Once stitched, turn the block to the back. Use the stitch lines as a guide to cut away the backing up to ¹/₄in (6mm) from the stitching line of the circle, revealing the freezer paper below. Ease up the fabric from the edge of the paper and pull the paper out. Press the completed block.

**24**  Add the inner framing strips to bring the block up to exactly 14 x 14in (35.6 x 35.6cm). Finally, add the sashing strips. See page 130 for instructions on framing and sashing.

# ALTERNATIVE DRUNKARD'S PATH

This is really a machine technique, using transparent thread as the top thread on the machine and the usual sewing thread in the bobbin. It can be stitched by hand, but if you can master this simple narrow zig-zag stitch you will find it really useful for projects where a more durable finish is needed. Exquisite hand appliqué is fine for your heirlooms but is not always suitable for children's quilts or lap quilts that are going to be used and possibly abused.

**Fig 1**

The Drunkard's Path block (Fig 1) consists of a square with a quarter circle or quadrant set into it. The radius of the quadrant is usually about two-thirds the length of the square (Fig 2). This method cheats in that the units are made four at a time. A complete circle is appliquéd onto a square and then cut into quarters to give the four Drunkard's Path units (Fig 3). The mathematical will soon spot that the completed units will not make true quarter circles as they lose a $1/4$in (6mm) when joined together. The only time this is at all noticeable is when two units are joined to make a semicircle (Fig 4a) or when four units make a complete circle (Fig 4b), as there are slight irregularities in the curve at the seams.

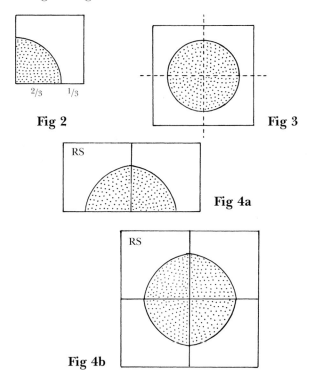

**Fig 2**

**Fig 3**

**Fig 4a**

**Fig 4b**

With this technique it is possible to make small Drunkard's Path units, which would not be so easy if the curves were pieced in the traditional way. I have chosen a design of thirty-six units, six in each row. Only twenty-eight are made up of the curved pieces, as eight whole squares are part of the design (Fig 1).

## COLOUR CHOICES

Three fabrics have been used for the design, which is set on a fourth fabric as the background around the outer edge. Choose fabrics where there is enough difference to allow the curved edges of the design to be seen.

### Setting up the Machine for Invisible Appliqué

Of course this is not completely invisible, but it is not an obvious edging like satin stitch – the better you get at it, the less it notices. You will need a finer needle when using transparent thread on the machine, a size 70 or 11. The transparent thread has got finer and easier to use in recent years. If the fabric of your circle is very pale, use the clear transparent thread. If using medium or dark fabric, choose the smoke-tinted thread. Beware of letting the loose end of thread unravel in your sewing box – it can come off the reel in handfuls if given the slightest opportunity. Stick the end on to the reel when it is not in use with a piece of masking tape. If you are not sure whether a type of nylon thread is suitable, take a thread of it and try to break it with your fingers. If it breaks easily then it will be safe to use and will not damage your fabric. As one American quilter succinctly put it, 'If it snaps, use it; if it doesn't, fish with it. . .'

Thread the machine with the transparent thread as the top thread. Use a normal thread in the bobbin in a colour that matches your square of fabric. You will need either to tighten the bottom tension or loosen the top tension so that when you stitch, the transparent thread does not pull the bottom thread up to the top surface where it could show on the fabric and spoil the effect. Do a practice piece to test this before starting on the actual block. Like machine piecing, it is a great help if you use an open-fronted foot on your machine so that you can see exactly what is happening ahead of the needle. The zig-zag used is so slight a swing that it is possible to use the special $1/4$in (6mm) patchwork foot that several of the sewing machine companies make without breaking the needle. Set the machine to a short stitch length of about $1^{1}/_{2}$ and a narrow zig-zag. I recommend starting with a stitch zig-zag width of 1 and edging it down narrower as you get more experienced. Unfortunately many of the all-singing, all-dancing computerised sewing machines jump from stitch width 1 down to 0.5 with no steps in between, so sometimes it is an advantage to have an old steam-driven model! If your machine hates the transparent thread, try using a normal top thread in a colour to match the fabric of the circle as this may well be successful.

## CONSTRUCTION

The design is based on square units which measure 2in (5cm) final size after stitching. To reach this measurement after all the stitching and cutting, the chosen final measurement of the square must be doubled and then 1in (2.5cm) added. Thus for this particular sizing the *starting* squares need to be cut 5 x 5in (12.7 x 12.7cm).

The radius of the quarter-circle used for the design is 1½in (3.9cm) final size, slightly more than two-thirds of the square unit, as I found it

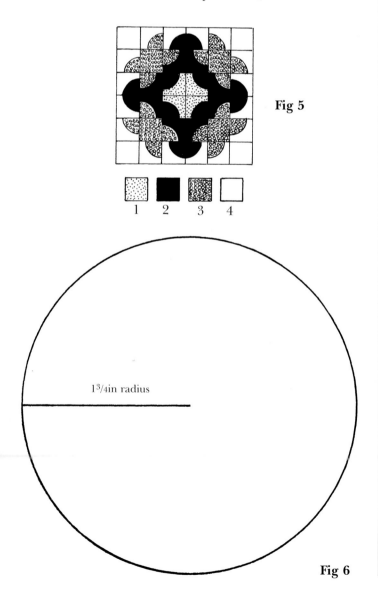

**Fig 5**

**Fig 6**

looked more effective. The radius of the circle used to make four of these at once needs to be ¼in (6mm) bigger which is 1¾in (4.5cm) (Fig 6).

### *Cutting the Squares*

**1** Fig 5 shows the design with the fabrics numbered below it. Cut the following squares:
From fabric 1, cut one square 5 x 5in (12.7 x 12.7cm).
From fabric 2, cut two squares each 5 x 5in (12.7 x 12.7cm).
From fabric 3, cut four smaller squares each 2½ x 2½in (6.3 x 6.3cm).
From the background fabric 4, cut four squares each 5 x 5in (12.7 x 12.7cm) and four smaller squares each 2½ x 2½in (6.3 x 6.3cm).

### *Cutting the Circles*

**2** Trace the circle in Fig 6 on to the non-shiny side of freezer paper seven times, or use a pair of compasses to draw seven circles each with a radius of 1¾in (4.5cm) on to the freezer paper. Cut out each circle on the drawn line.
**3** Take a piece of fabric 2 (do not use the cut squares for this). Set the iron to a wool setting with no steam and use a firm ironing surface to iron three paper circles shiny side down on to the *wrong* side of this fabric, leaving at least ½in (1.2cm) between each circle to allow for the ¼in (6mm) seam allowances. Cut out each circle, adding a ¼in (6mm) seam allowance as in Fig 7.

In the same way, iron the other four paper circles on to the *wrong* side of fabric 3. Cut out each circle, adding ¼in (6mm) seam allowance.
**4** Peel one paper circle off the fabric and replace it shiny side *up* on the *wrong* side of the fabric circle in exactly the same position leaving the ¼in (6mm) seam allowance on all sides. Pin the freezer paper on to the fabric. I use two pins to stop the paper moving (Fig 8). Using the side of the iron rather than the point, nudge the seam allowance of fabric over on to the freezer paper,

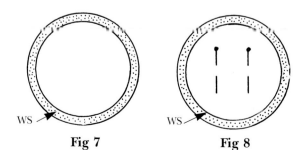

**Fig 7**     **Fig 8**

COLLIE PARKER

*'The discipline of working with a restricted palette proved to be a difficult challenge.
However, the quilt came to life with the addition of the sashing colour.'*

easing in the fullness a little at a time until all the seam allowance is stuck down on the paper. Take care not to press any tiny pleats in the outer edge but keep the curve smooth (Fig 9). Repeat this process with the remaining six circles. Remove the pins.

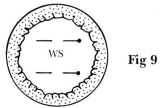

**Fig 9**

**5** Arrange the fabric circles on the cut 5 x 5in (12.7 x 12.7cm) squares as shown in Fig 10. To help position the circles accurately, trace the circle and surrounding square from Fig 11 on to tracing paper. Cut out the square exactly on the drawn line. Remove the centre circle section by cutting on the drawn line of the circle (Fig 12). If you place the tracing paper on a square of fabric,

**Fig 10**

matching the corners and edges carefully, the fabric circle can be positioned in the centre hole. The square of fabric should be lying right side *up* when the circle is placed on it. Turn the circle so that the grain of the fabric matches the

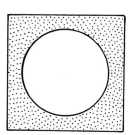

**Fig 12**

grain-line marked on the paper square. Press the circle with an iron to fix it onto the fabric square. You may also want to pin it in place.

***Stitching the Circle on the Square***

**6** Once you have set your machine up for invisible appliqué (see page 125), position the fabric on the machine so that the *left* swing of the needle stitches into the very edge of the appliqué (the circle) (Fig 13a), and the *right* swing of the needle stitches just off the appliqué in the ditch between appliqué and background (Fig 13b).

**7** Start to stitch, taking it very slowly to start with. Do not worry if you miss catching the appliqué occasionally. If a gap is noticeable you can patch it by stitching that section a second time. Try not to stitch both left and right swings of the zig-zag up on the

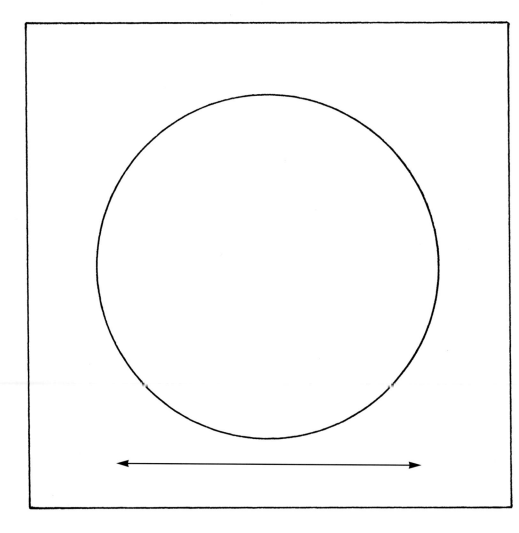

**Fig 11**

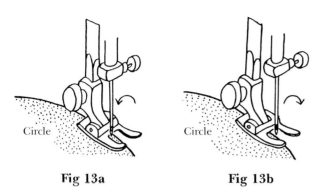

**Fig 13a**          **Fig 13b**

appliqué, as this flattens the edge and you lose the soft-edged effect. Transparent thread can easily come undone, so usually the stitches need to be secured at either end of the appliqué by stitching several stitches in reverse. As this design is a continuous curved edge, just begin stitching and when you get round to the starting point again, stitch over the beginning stitches for about 1/2in (1.2cm) to secure them.

### Sewing the Curve by Hand

If for any reason you are not happy with this machine technique, or just because you prefer handwork, the edge of the circle can be appliquéd by hand, like the circles in the Clamshell block. Because the circle will later be cut into four, it is best not to stitch across these cutting lines. Press and pin the circle onto the fabric square. Place the square on a cutting board and use a rotary ruler to find the halfway point on each side. This is where the block will be cut after stitching. Mark the edges of the circle in these four places (Fig 14). Stitch the circle in place, stitching each quarter circle separately so that when the circle is cut into quarters the stitching will not come undone.

**8** Once all seven circles are stitched into position, either by hand or machine, turn each square of fabric to the back and use the stitch lines as a guide to cut away the backing up to 1/4in (6mm) from the stitching line of the circle, revealing the freezer paper below. Ease up the fabric from the edge of the paper and pull the paper out.

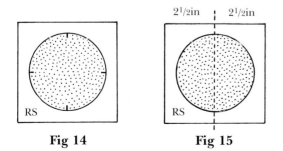

**Fig 14**            **Fig 15**

**9** Press each unit from the front and place one on a cutting board. Use the markings on the board and a rotary ruler to find the midline on the square, 2 1/2in (6.3cm) from each edge (Fig 15). Cut the square in half vertically on this line.

**10** Take each half square and place it on the cutting board as in Fig 16. Find the midline as shown in Fig 16 and cut each piece along this line to give four quarters (Fig 17). Repeat this process with the other six squares. You should finish up with twenty-eight quarter units, each measuring 2 1/2 x 2 1/2in (6.3 x 6.3cm).

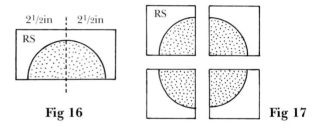

**Fig 16**            **Fig 17**

**11** Combine these with the eight squares measuring 2 1/2 x 2 1/2in (6.3 x 6.3cm) cut earlier and arrange them to make the design in Fig 5 (page 126). If you prefer an alternative layout, arrange the pieces until you are happy with the design.

**12** Stitch the squares of the top row together. Match the two edges of the circle section on squares 3 and 4 very carefully (Fig 18). There are only four places in the design where this match has to be made, so it is worth taking the time to get it right. Press the seams to one side, ironing from the front of the work.

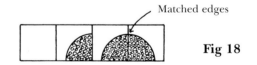

Matched edges

**Fig 18**

**13** Stitch the squares of row two together. Press the seams in the opposite direction to those of row one, ironing from the front. Join rows one and two, matching seams carefully. Stitch the squares of row three together and press the seams in the opposite direction to those of row two. Pin and stitch this row to row two, matching seams carefully.

Continue to stitch together the squares, row by row, and join them to the block until all six rows are joined. Press the completed block from the front of the work.

**14** Add the inner framing strips and trim the block to an exact 14in (35.6cm) square. Finally, add the sashing strips. See page 130 for instructions on framing and sashing.

# FINISHING AND QUILTING THE BLOCKS

### FRAMING AND SASHING

The blocks in this New Sampler Quilt are not all the same size as each other, which gives some flexibility to the maker. Once each block is completed it is trimmed if necessary and then an inner framing border is added to bring the block up to 14 x 14in (35.6 x 35.6cm) (Fig 1). The block is then sashed with strips and an added feature made with a square of different fabric in each opposite corner (Fig 2). When the blocks are joined, these squares become units of four at each junction, called a Four-Patch (Fig 3).

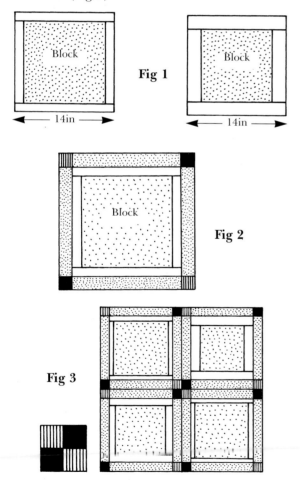

**Fig 1**

**Fig 2**

**Fig 3**

I used a variety of fabrics for my inner frame (see picture, page 2), but many others used the same fabric throughout. About 1¼yd (115cm) in total is needed for the inner frame and about 2yd (182.8cm) for all the sashing strips. If possible, cut all the strips down the length of the fabric parallel with the selvedge edge as it is less stretchy.

### *Adding the Inner Framing Strips*

The block plus inner frame must measure 14 x 14in (35.6 x 35.6cm) *exactly*, including the outer raw edges.

**1** Trim the block to a regular square. Do not trim off part of the design and lose corners or points. If necessary use a steam iron to press the block into a regular shape, checking this by placing it on to a cutting board between pressings and using the drawn grid on the board as a guide. The sides need to be vertical and the top and bottom edges horizontal – this seems obvious but it is amazing how many people can ignore this basic requirement.

Blocks that have a central design set in a background need only to be trimmed into a regular square to a size that suits the design before the framing strips are added.

**2** The table at the top of page 131 gives the width of strips needed for an inner frame to bring the block up to exactly 14 x 14in (35.6 x 35.6cm). Do not take a long strip and just stitch it on, trimming the end after stitching. The edges of the block may well stretch as you stitch and will no longer measure a true square when you finish. Cut the framing strips to size and make the block fit them exactly. (If your block does not match exactly the measurements given in the table, see Adding Inner Framing Strips to a Block with an Odd Measurement, on page 131.)

**3** Pin and stitch the first two strips to the sides of the block (Fig 4). Make the block fit the strips exactly. Press the seams outwards from the block, ironing from the front of the work. The block should now measure 14in (35.6cm) from side to side. If somehow it has turned out wider, trim it down to exactly the right size. If it is smaller, check your seam allowance. I'm afraid your seams probably need to be restitched, taking a narrower seam allowance.

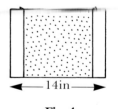

**Fig 4**

## FRAMING STRIPS FOR BLOCKS

| Block Measurement | Measurement of Framing Strips |
|---|---|
| $11^{1/2}$ x $11^{1/2}$in (29.2 x 29.2cm) cut size | two strips $11^{1/2}$ x $1^{3/4}$in (29.2 x 4.5cm)<br>two strips 14 x $1^{3/4}$in (35.6 x 4.5cm |
| $11^{3/4}$ x $11^{3/4}$in (29.8 x 29.8cm) cut size | two strips $11^{3/4}$ x $1^{5/8}$in (29.8 x 4.1cm)<br>two strips 14 x $1^{5/8}$in (35.6 x 4.1cm |
| 12 x 12in (30.5 x 30.5cm) cut size | two strips 12 x $1^{1/2}$in (30.5 x 3.9cm)<br>two strips 14 x $1^{1/2}$in (35.6 x 3.9cm |
| $12^{1/4}$ x $12^{1/4}$in (31.1 x 31.1cm) cut size | two strips $12^{1/4}$ x $1^{3/8}$in (31.1 x 3.5cm)<br>two strips 14 x $1^{3/8}$in (35.6 x 3.5cm) |
| $12^{1/2}$ x $12^{1/2}$in (31.7 x 31.7cm) cut size | two strips $12^{1/2}$ x $1^{1/4}$in (31.7 x 3.2cm)<br>two strips 14 x $1^{1/4}$in (35.6 x 3.2cm) |
| $12^{3/4}$ x $12^{3/4}$in (32.4 x 32.4cm) cut size | two strips $12^{3/4}$ x $1^{1/8}$in (32.4 x 2.8cm)<br>two strips 14 x $1^{1/8}$in (35.6 x 2.8cm) |
| 13 x 13cm (33 x 33cm) cut size | two strips 13 x 1in (33 x 2.5cm)<br>two strips 14 x 1in (35.6 x 2.5cm) |
| $13^{1/4}$ x $13^{1/4}$in (33.6 x 33.6cm) cut size | two strips $13^{1/4}$ x $7/8$in (33.6 x 2.2cm)<br>two strips 14 x $7/8$in (35.6 x 2.2cm) |
| $13^{1/2}$ x $13^{1/2}$in (34.3 x 34.3cm) cut size | two strips $13^{1/2}$ x $3/4$in (34.3 x 1.9cm)<br>two strips 14 x $3/4$in (35.6 x 1.9cm) |

**4** Cut two framing strips in the same width as the first pair and 14in (35.6cm) in length. Pin and stitch these to the top and bottom of the block (Fig 5). Press the seams outwards, ironing from the front of the block.

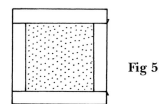

**Fig 5**

### Adding Inner Framing Strips to a Block with an Odd Measurement

If your trimmed and pressed block doesn't match exactly one of the measurements in the table, don't worry. The only thing that matters is that the sides are vertical and the top and bottom edges are horizontal.
**1** Place the block on a cutting board and check that the edges are parallel with the drawn lines on the board. More trimming or steaming may be needed to get this correct. Measure the block from top to bottom down its centre. Find the block in the table with a measurement nearest to yours but *larger*. Use the width measurement given in the table for your own strips.
**2** Cut two strips in this width and in a length to

match your own block. Pin and stitch these strips to either side of the block (Fig 4). Press the seams outwards, pressing from the front of the block.
**3** Place the block on the cutting board and trim the side strips down equally on both sides so that the block measures exactly 14in (35.6cm) from side to side (Fig 4).
**4** Cut two framing strips in the same width as the first pair and 14in (35.6cm) in length. Pin and stitch these to the top and bottom of the block (Fig 5). Press the seams outwards, ironing from the front of the block.

### Adding the Sashing Strips

**1** For each block cut four strips of the fabric chosen for the sashing, each measuring 14 x $1^{3/4}$in (35.6 x 4.5cm). Two more fabrics are needed to make the Four-Patch that appears at each junction of blocks. Each of these squares measures $1^{3/4}$ x $1^{3/4}$in (4.5 x 4.5cm).
**2** Pin and stitch the sashing strips to each side of the block (Fig 6, page 132). Press the seams outwards, ironing from the front of the work.
**3** To either end of a sashing strip stitch a square of Four-Patch fabric with one fabric used at one end and the other fabric at the other (Fig 7). Press the seams from the front towards the long strip. Repeat this with the remaining sashing strip.

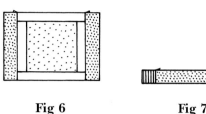

**Fig 6**                    **Fig 7**

**4** Pin and stitch one sashing strip with its end squares (called cornerstones) to the top of the block, matching seams carefully (Fig 8).

**5** Pin and stitch the other sashing strip to the bottom of the block with the two cornerstones in opposite corners to the first pair (Fig 9). Press the seams outwards from the front. Each block should now measure exactly 16½ x 16½in (41.9 x 41.9cm). As you sash each framed block take care that the same cornerstone fabric is always in the top left-hand corner, or your little Four-Patch design will not work out. Some blocks can be turned through 90° to correct a mistake, but alas, not all of them, so make sure the blocks are the right way up when the cornerstones are added in their correct position.

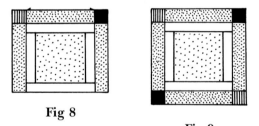

**Fig 8**

**Fig 9**

## QUILTING THE BLOCKS

Once a quilt is pieced together it is backed with another fabric and often an extra layer of padding is sandwiched between front and back. This layer is kept in place with decorative patterns of stitches known as quilting. Hand quilting is a running stitch which makes a broken line of stitches, giving a subtle effect to the quilting design. Machine quilting has a more defined look as the stitches form a continuous line. There is no reason why both hand and machine quilting should not be combined in a quilt. I hand-quilted most of my New Sampler Quilt and machine-quilted in the seams of the inner frames and sashing around each block.

It is likely that many people tackling this New Sampler Quilt will have had some experience of quilting and already know whether hand or machine work is what they do best and, most important, what gives them pleasure. I like to do hand quilting where it will show on the quilt and enhance the design. Machine quilting I use for stitching in the seamlines (called quilting in the ditch) where it defines the piecing without being noticeable. Hand quilting in seams is quite difficult because of the extra layers and does not show on the quilt, so I avoid it.

Just as the quilt gives an opportunity to try new techniques in the blocks, so it is a good chance to explore and develop quilting skills. Sheila Barton's quilt shown in this section of the book on page 137 is one of the few that is entirely machine-quilted with much surface stitch decoration, which hopefully will encourage us all to sit at the machine on a wet afternoon and *practise*.

Shirley Prescott's quilt on page 102 is also machine-quilted, most of it in the ditch, so that the block designs are well-defined. Hand quilting takes forever to do, but soothes my soul. If you do not enjoy the hand work or you are short of time, work at the machine quilting.

### *Preparing the Blocks for Quilting*

It is very convenient to quilt each block individually as they are easy to take around for hand quilting and a good size to work on at the machine. Some students finished all the blocks, chose the final arrangement and then joined them in rows. Each row was then quilted and the rows joined together afterwards. A few preferred to join all the blocks, add the borders and then quilt the entire piece.

For each block (or larger area if you have chosen to join several blocks before quilting) cut a piece of batting and backing fabric each measuring ½in (1.2cm) larger on all sides than the completed block. For a single block this will be 17 x 17in (43.2 x 43.2cm). Layer the backing fabric (right side

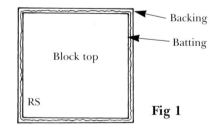

**Fig 1**

down) with the batting and the block placed centrally on it with right side upwards (Fig 1).

If hand quilting, tack the layers together with running stitches ¾–1in (1.9–2.5cm) long, using a long, fine needle. Work from the centre of the block outwards in a grid of vertical and horizontal lines about 3–4in (7.6–10cm) apart (Fig 2).

If machine quilting, use 1in (2.5cm) safety pins

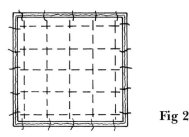

Fig 2

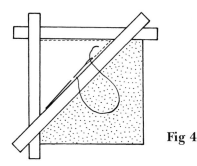

Fig 4

at a distance of 3–4in (7.6–10cm) over the block. Tacking stitches are not suitable when machine quilting as they catch in the feet while stitching. Keep the pins well clear of the areas to be quilted so that they do not get in the way of the machine foot as it stitches.

### Where to Quilt?

Traditionally, hand quilting echoes the lines of the patchwork not in the seam itself but 1/4in (6mm) away from it, called outline quilting (Fig 3), while machine quilting is more often in the seam itself. Large areas can be broken up with extra lines or curves which add interest. Do not quilt in the sashing on the block as you will need to fold this part back when joining the blocks together. Study the blocks shown in the quilt photographs throughout the book to get inspiration. Each block should be quilted roughly the same amount, so don't quilt extensively on the first block unless you are prepared to do the same for all twenty blocks.

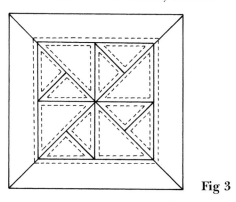

Fig 3

### Marking the Design

I try to avoid marking a quilt with pencil lines as much as possible. Outline quilting lines, which are usually 1/4in (6mm) away from the seamlines, can be sewn by eye or by using 1/4in (6mm) low-tack masking tape. Stick the tape lightly to the surface of the top fabric with one edge against the seamline. Quilt close to the other edge and remove the tape immediately the stitching has been completed (Fig 4).

Curved designs can be made by placing glasses,

saucers or plates on the fabric and marking around the edge. I marked all the quilting designs on my New Sampler Quilt using a ruler with 1/4in (6mm) markings, a set of acrylic circles in various sizes and a marking tool called a hera. This is a gem of a tool that I recommend to all quilters. It has an edge rather like a butter knife that makes a sharp crease in the fabric when drawn firmly across its surface. It works well against the edge of a ruler to give straight lines for quilting and even round a curved edge. The line lasts as long as you need it and can be removed just by damping the fabric slightly and letting it dry naturally. If I need to mark with a pencil I use watercolour pencils from an art shop in a colour that tones with the fabric. This wears away in time and washes out.

## QUILTING BY HAND

The technique of hand quilting is dealt with fully in *The Sampler Quilt Book* (see Bibliography, page 143) but the basics are also described here briefly.

### Tacking the Layers

First place the batting on the backing fabric and then the block centrally on the batting. Use a long, fine needle and light-coloured tacking thread and tack the layers together using running stitches 3/4–1in (1.9–2.5cm) long. Work from the centre of the block outwards across the quilt in a grid of vertical and horizontal lines.

### Using a Frame

When quilting, I would recommend the use of one of the newer, square plastic frames, as they make a convenient shape to fit around the blocks. A tacked block should never be stretched tightly in the frame – adjust the side clips so the fabric has some 'give', which will make quilting easier. A frame is virtually essential for quilting large pieces.

### Starting to Quilt

Begin by cutting a length of quilting thread about 18in (45.7cm) long. This can be a contrasting colour to your fabric or a shade to blend with the colours of the block. Begin quilting in the centre of the block and work outwards. All starting and finishing is done from the top of the quilt, so make a knot at one end of the thread and push the needle into the top fabric and batting (not the backing) 1in (2.5cm) away from the starting point, preferably further along the line you are going to quilt. Bring the needle back up to the surface in position to make the first stitch, which I make a backstitch. Pull gently to pop the knot through the top fabric into the batting.

### The Quilting Stitch

Begin quilting each time with a backstitch and a space so that it appears to be a running stitch. When you first quilt it may be easier to make one stitch at a time but with practice you can increase this. It doesn't matter if your stitches are not as small as you would like: what is important is that the stitches are the same size. This becomes easier as you keep stitching and establish a rhythm. Check the back occasionally to ensure that the stitches are being made on that side as well, but don't expect them to be exactly the same size. They are usually smaller, and as long as you are catching in enough of the back fabric to hold it securely in place that will be fine.

If you are quilting without a frame, it is possible to hold the fabric between the thumb and finger of one hand while quilting with the other, to manoeuvre the layers. To make the running quilting stitch a reasonable size on the back and front, the needle must be pushed into the work as vertically as possible and then swung upwards. This is why it's best to use Betweens needles, as they are short and strong and won't bend too easily. I use the top of a thimble to swing the needle up and down.

Watch the tension of your stitches by pulling the thread to tighten the stitches just enough to draw the top fabric down but not so much that it puckers. When quilting without a frame, always work from the centre outwards. It may be easier to use several threads at the same time while doing this. If you turn and quilt back towards the middle you may finish up with a bulge or a twist in the fabric in the centre.

If quilting *with* a frame you need a different approach because the fabric cannot be gathered and held between your thumb and finger while quilting. Place your free hand under the quilt, with the top of your middle finger in the area where the needle should come through the quilt. Rest the top

of the needle against the flat end of the thimble and push the needle vertically through the layers until the tip is just (and only just) touching the underneath finger. Press the layers down ahead of the needle with the thumb of your sewing hand.

Push the tip of the needle upwards with the underneath finger. At the same time use the thimble to swing the needle head over and forward to help bring the needle tip to the surface.

Swing the head of the needle upwards to make the next stitch until it is almost vertical, and push down with the thimble until the needle tip touches the underneath finger.

Again, use a combination of the underneath finger and the thumb in front of the needle to help force the needle up to the surface of the work while you swing the needle head down on to the quilt top with the thimble. This rocking action can be repeated to make as many stitches on the needle as are comfortable. Pull the needle through the layers, giving a slight tug on the thread to pull the stitches snugly on to the quilt top. Continue in this way until the quilting is complete.

To finish off, either make a knot in the thread close to the surface of the fabric or wind the thread twice round the needle and insert the needle into the batting, running it at least 1in (2.5cm) away from the stitching. Pull gently to pop the knot beneath the surface of the top fabric. Cut off the thread level with the quilt top.

I use this same technique to move from one part of the design to emerge at another. Finish with a knot, run the thread through the batting and emerge at the new stitching line. Remember to always begin with a backstitch before continuing to quilt.

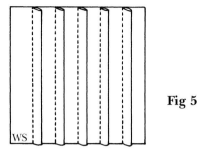

**Fig 5**

### QUILTING BY MACHINE

One of the most important preliminaries to machine quilting is to get your sewing area comfortable and efficient to work in. I have an office chair that I can adjust to a comfortable height for machine work and sit at a large table with a good light. Beware of working too long at the machine and getting an aching neck or shoulders through tension.

The top thread can be either normal sewing thread to tone with the quilt or the invisible thread described in the Alternative Drunkard's Path block (page 125). Use the normal thread in the bobbin in a colour to match the backing fabric and use a size 9 or 70 needle for invisible thread or a 12 or 80 for normal thread. Try the stitches on a practice piece to check that top and bottom tensions are equally balanced. Use a stitch length that pleases the eye, about the same as for dressmaking or possibly slightly longer.

#### *Quilting in the Ditch*

Unless your machine has dual-feed you will need to buy a walking foot for this. These can be expensive but are invaluable for stitching evenly through layers of fabric and batting. Practise stitching first on a trial sample. Take a piece of plain fabric and stitch several straight pleats in it (Fig 5), using the side of the machine foot as a measurement – you can use the walking foot for this if it is fitted or your usual sewing foot. Turn the fabric over and press the pleats to one side. The seams made can be used for practice in ditch-stitching. Layer a piece of backing fabric, batting and the prepared seamed fabric and pin together ready for stitching. Aim to stitch as near to the seam as possible, stitching in the single layer of fabric which is lower than the other side. Try not to stitch up on the higher side of the seam, as this really notices.

*A machine quilted Attic Windows block by Sheila Barton*

135

Start and finish your stitches with a series of very short stitches, about six or seven of them. Leave long thread ends, about 4in (10cm), so that the top thread can be pulled through to the back of the work easily. Use a needle with a large eye to pull both threads into the batting for some distance. Trim off any ends that remain on the surface of the fabric. If you have a 'needle down' option on your machine, use it to keep the needle in position in the fabric when you pause to turn corners or adjust direction round a curve.

### Free Machine Quilting

For quilting very curved or complex designs the feed dogs are either dropped or covered so that the fabric is no longer forced along at an even pace. Read your machine instruction manual to see how to adjust your machine for this. Use the darning foot or a special extra-large free-machining foot that can be obtained from quilt shops to fit some machines.

To start, lower the presser foot in the place where you want to begin quilting. Hold on to the end of the top thread and make one stitch. Pull the thread to bring the bottom thread up through the quilt to the top. Hold both threads while you stitch the first few stitches, which should be a series of six or seven very short stitches. Stop, and snip the thread ends off close to the stitching.

Place your hands in a C-shape either side of the pressure foot and press down gently to move the layers of the quilt around while keeping the speed of the machine as consistent as you can. Aim to make even stitches of a uniform length. Finish by reducing the length of the last six or seven stitches to the smallest possible size.

To move to a new area, lift the presser foot and position it where you wish to begin stitching. Do not snip the threads, but keep them taut between the two areas. Lower the pressure foot and wind the needle into the quilt by hand. Start to quilt with the usual six to seven tiny stitches, then snip the connecting threads before continuing to stitch. Balancing speed and movement is the real skill and needs plenty of practise. Make up several trial pieces and work through stitching straight lines by eye, curves, writing your name and the overall scribbling effect known as vermicelli quilting. Like hand quilting, machine quilting improves with practise, so put in the time and your confidence and control of the machine will increase. Once you feel ready, start quilting the blocks. Begin with ditch-quilting and any outline quilting using the walking foot, then progress to free-machine quilting in the shapes of the design and finally any quilting to fill in the background areas if desired.

## JOINING THE BLOCKS

Joining the blocks together is not a difficult task but it can be tedious. Still, at least by this stage all the quilting is completed and the quilt starts taking shape like magic as each row is added. The method I use ensures that the joining seams on the back of the quilt reflect those on the front so that the back looks as neat and balanced as possible.

## CONSTRUCTION

**1** Arrange the completed blocks in your chosen design. Take your time over this and if possible get a second or third opinion, preferably from a fellow quilter. There may, of course, be a block that just does not fit in and you may have to be brave, discard it and make another. Sometimes, though, the block you have felt uneasy about since it was made fits in the final arrangement perfectly. Only at this stage, when all the blocks are laid out and the overall balance established, can you make these decisions.

**2** Take the blocks that will make up the top row of the quilt (Fig 1) and place the first two blocks to be joined right sides down. Pull the backing fabric and batting back from the vertical sides to be joined on each block front and pin them out of the way (Fig 2).

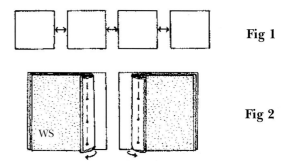

**Fig 1**

**Fig 2**

**3** With right sides facing, match and pin the two edges of the block fronts together. Machine-stitch them together with a 1/4in (6mm) seam allowance (Fig 3). Finger press the seam open and press it lightly with the point of an iron from the *front* of

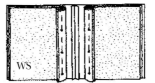

**Fig 3**

SHEILA BARTON

*'A length of black print cotton given as a present was the inspiration for my quilt. Other fabrics were bought to tone with it and this started my first major project and what was to become an addiction.'*

the work. If you try to press it on the back there is a danger of the iron touching the batting and melting it.

**4** Lay the joined blocks right sides down on a flat surface. Unpin the batting, but leave the backing fabric pinned back out of the way. Let the two edges of batting overlap each other and cut through both layers along the centre so that the final cut edges butt together. It does not matter exactly where this cut is made as it will be hidden by the fabric. If you are nervous about accidentally cutting the front of the blocks, slide an ordinary 12in (30.5cm) ruler between the batting and the block front before you cut so that your scissors cannot come into contact with the block beneath (Fig 4).

**5** Keep the ruler between the layers while you stitch the two butted edges of batting together. I use a large herringbone stitch as it helps to keep the edges flat (Fig 5).

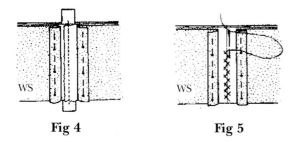

**Fig 4**                    **Fig 5**

**6** Remove the ruler and turn over the joined blocks so that they are now right sides upwards. Push a line of pins through the joining seam and batting from the front. They should be pushed right through so that their points stand upright when the quilt blocks are turned over (Fig 6a). Avoid using glass-headed pins for this task, as the heads roll sideways and prevent the pins from remaining upright.

**7** Turn the blocks over with the backing fabric facing upwards (Fig 6b). Fold each piece of backing fabric so that the folded edge butts up to the line of pins. Finger press the fold and trim any excess fabric to the 1/4in (6mm) seam allowance (Fig 6c).

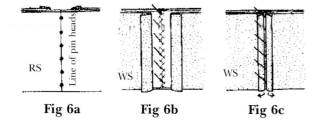

**Fig 6a**        **Fig 6b**        **Fig 6c**

**8** Remove the pins. Unfold the backing fabric of block one and smooth it flat on the batting (Fig 7a). Unfold the backing fabric of block two and *re-fold* it so that the seam allowance is turned under. Match the fold of block two to the creased line of block one (Fig 7b). Pin together, again putting a ruler under the seam, this time to avoid sewing into the batting.

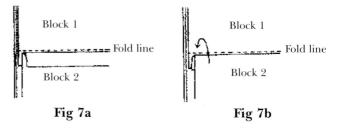

**Fig 7a**                    **Fig 7b**

**9** Sew along the overlapping seam with a slip stitch or blind hemming stitch. You can remove the ruler to sew most of this seam, but keep it in place for the first and final 2in (5cm). It does not matter if the stitches penetrate the batting along this seam in the middle areas, but the end 2in (5cm) have to be kept in separate layers so that they can be joined to the next row of blocks (Fig 8).

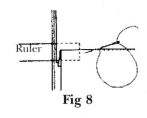

**Fig 8**

**10** Repeat this process to join all the blocks in the top row. Check that the backing fabric is not pulled too tight and that the front sashing strips are well matched and lying flat. Adjust the back seams if they are pulling too tightly.

**11** Join the blocks in each horizontal row in the same way (Fig 9). Now join those horizontal rows in exactly the same way, matching seams and borders carefully (Fig 10). The quilt is now ready for its borders and final binding.

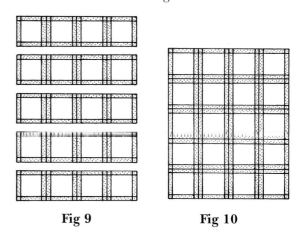

**Fig 9**                    **Fig 10**

# COMPLETING THE QUILT

## BORDERS

When the quilt top has been joined together you need to think about the borders. Put the quilt on the bed to see how wide the borders need to be. If it is just going to cover the top of the bed like an eiderdown, it may not need any extra borders.

I began my New Sampler Quilt as the teaching sample for the course, but as it went on I loved it more and more and determined to use it for the next twenty years or more on our brass bed. I had planned to add two simple framing borders, but found that I needed more than this to cover the bed base and look good, so here was a chance to add a border design that I had been admiring for ages. More work, more quilting and a very large quilt to carry around to classes and exhibitions, but an addition that I am really pleased with (see picture, page 2).

Study all the photographs in this book – all quilts made by genuine students trying out the New Sampler Quilt course. Some have rich and complex borders, others a simple double border of complementary fabrics which set off the quilt beautifully. As always, the choice of borders is yours and yours alone.

You may be severely restricted in your choice of fabrics by this time. Pieced borders using all the left-over scraps may be the answer, or you could use totally new fabrics. It doesn't matter if a fabric has not been used in the quilt, as long as it looks as though it belongs. The light fabric used around the edge of the pieced border on my quilt is not in the main quilt at all. I had just half a metre of it and was so short of fabric that one of the small squares in the corners is made up from several joined scraps. A *real* patchwork quilt!

Plain borders cry out to be quilted, although wide patterned borders, if they form the drop down each side of the bed, can look good without quilting. If you have really had enough by this time then add simple borders and keep quilting to a minimum.

At this stage it is easiest to make the borders and join them to the front of the quilt only and not to the batting and backing. Ignore the back until all the extra pieces – apart from the final binding – have been added to the quilt top.

### STRIP BORDERS
A simple framing border of one or more strips of fabric is very effective (Fig 1). If there is not enough fabric to cut strips for the length of the quilt, you can get away with a few joins, provided they are placed midway in the border or at regular intervals so that they look planned. If you do not have any suitable fabric left for the border you may have to go out and buy something special. It may seem an extravagance at this stage, but any fabric left over will always come in useful for a future project. Another excuse to buy more fabric. . .

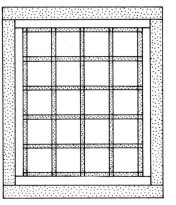

**Fig 1**

### CONSTRUCTION
**1** Lay the quilt top on a flat surface and measure its length down the *centre*, not the edge (Fig 2). If you always do this and cut the borders to match the centre measurements there is less danger of the quilt edges spreading to give wavy borders.
**2** Cut two strips of border fabric in the chosen width to match the quilt measurement – these will make the side borders. Pin back the batting and backing fabric out of the way and pin and stitch each side strip to the quilt top, easing in any fullness in the quilt. Work on a flat surface and match the centres and both ends before pinning the rest. Press the seams outwards, away from the quilt (Fig 3).
**3** Measure the quilt from side to side across the centre (Fig 4). Cut two strips of border fabric in

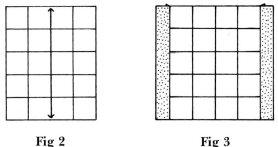

**Fig 2**          **Fig 3**

the chosen width to match this measurement. Pin and stitch these to the top and bottom of the quilt, matching centres and both ends and avoiding the batting and backing fabric as before (Fig 5). Press the seams outwards away from the quilt top.

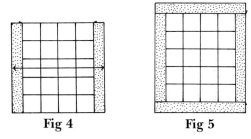

**Fig 4**          **Fig 5**

**4** If another border is planned, measure the quilt down its centre and repeat the process, sides first and then top and bottom (Fig 1).

**5** You may prefer to make your borders with cornerstones, which echo the squares linking the sashing strips. Measure the quilt across its centre in *both* directions and cut strips of the chosen width to match these measurements. Stitch the side strips to the quilt as usual. Press the seams outwards away from the quilt. Cut four squares of fabric for the cornerstones the same size as the cut width of the border strips. Stitch one of these to either end of both top and bottom border strips (Fig 6). Press the seams towards the long strip. Pin and stitch these border strips to the top and bottom of the quilt, matching seams carefully (Fig 7). Press the seams outwards, away from the quilt. If a second border with cornerstones is planned, re-measure the quilt after the first border is added and repeat the process (Fig 8).

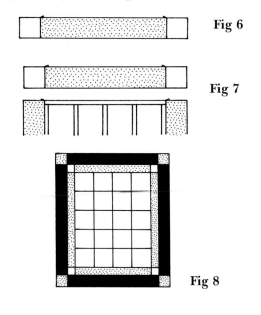

**Fig 6**

**Fig 7**

**Fig 8**

## PIECED BORDERS

Pieced borders made from scraps are an ideal way to use up spare fabric and can greatly enrich your quilt. At this stage the outer edge of the quilt will have only one width of sashing strip around it. With a busy pieced border you may find that a second sashing width needs to be added to the quilt, and possibly even another wider border strip beyond this, before the pieced border is stitched in place. If this is the case, follow the instructions for adding strip borders given earlier.

Both squares and rectangles can be used to make a pieced border. Figs 9 and 10 show suggested designs for using cut squares: 2½in (6.3cm) cut squares are a comfortable size and should fit mathematically around the quilt.

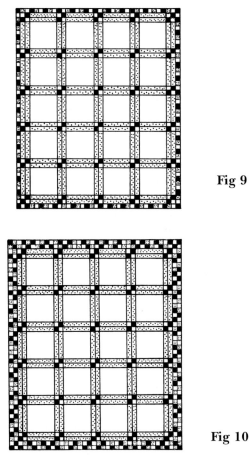

**Fig 9**

**Fig 10**

If not, position a seam at the centre of the quilt and trim the two ends to make matching rectangles (Fig 11). Fig 12 shows a design using 2½in (6.3cm) rectangles, cut any length you like, around the quilt.

**Fig 11**

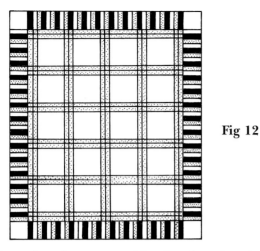

**Fig 12**

Several students created borders based on larger versions of techniques that feature in the blocks, such as Delectable Mountains or Folded Flying Geese. My own border was based on half-square and quarter-square triangles (Fig 13).

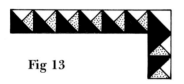

**Fig 13**

It is not always possible to make repeat designs for border strips in an exact measurement to fit the quilt. My design was based on a 3in (7.6cm) repeat which had to go continuously around the quilt, including turning the corners.

One solution is to make the border strips and try them against the quilt as they grow. It may be that by adjusting a few seams or by some creative pressing with a steam iron the border can be made to fit the quilt. I solved the problem with my own quilt by making the borders first and then adding an extra framing strip all around the quilt itself to bring it up to the correct size to fit the borders. Regular repeat designs like Flying Geese can be broken at the corners and midway, where spacing pieces can be inserted to make the sizing correct (Fig 14).

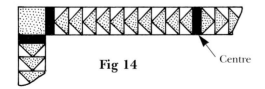

**Fig 14**    Centre

You may want to add another frame beyond the pieced border. Lay the quilt top on a flat surface and measure it again. Work from these measurements when cutting the new strips. If you keep a tight control on the length of each border strip as you add it, you will finish up with a beautifully flat quilt without a hint of a wave or ripple.

### BACKING THE BORDERS

Once all the borders have been added to the quilt top, extra batting and backing fabric must be added which extends at least ¹/₂in (1.2cm) beyond the quilt on all sides. Join the batting with herringbone stitch along the butted edges in the same way as when joining the blocks (see page 138). Strips of the backing fabric can then be machine-stitched to the back of the quilt to make it the same size as the batting. Join the side pieces first and then the top and bottom strips. Press the seams outwards as usual.

Any quilting in the border areas should be done at this stage, tacking the layers together thoroughly before quilting. Although the quilt is cumbersome now, at least the extra quilting is all around the edge so should not be too difficult to get at.

### BINDING THE QUILT

I suggest making double-fold binding for the quilt. Strips are cut on the straight grain of the fabric and have two thicknesses on the folded edge, making it more durable. Mitred corners are not necessary as there are no mitres in the blocks or sashing.

### CONSTRUCTION

**1** Before adding the final binding, check that the quilt lies flat and the corners are really square. Tacking with small stitches near to the edge of the quilt will help keep the quilt flat and avoid wavy edges. Trim the batting and backing fabric down to exactly ¹/₄in (6mm) beyond the quilt top (Fig 1).

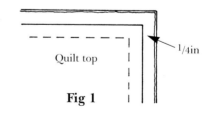

Quilt top    1/4in

**Fig 1**

**2** Cut four strips of fabric for the binding, each 2¹/₂in (6.3cm) wide. The two side strips should measure the length of the quilt from top to bottom. The two strips for the top and bottom edges should measure the width of the quilt from side to side plus 1¹/₂in (3.8cm). Shorter lengths can be joined if you do not have enough fabric.
**3** Take each side binding strip and fold it in half, right side *outwards*, without pressing. Pin a folded strip to one side of the quilt, matching the edges

(Fig 2). Stitch a seam ¼in (6mm) from the edge of the quilt top through all the layers (Fig 3). Repeat this with the second strip on the other side of the quilt.

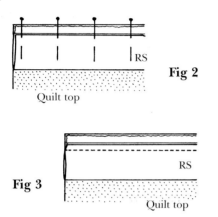

**Fig 2**

Quilt top

**Fig 3**

RS

Quilt top

**4** Bring the folded edge of the binding over to the back and stitch in place by hand, just covering the line of machine stitches (Fig 4).

**Fig 4**

Quilt back

**5** Pin and stitch the folded binding to the top and bottom of the quilt in the same way, leaving about ¾in (1.9cm) of binding extending beyond the quilt at each end (Fig 5). Trim this back to about ½in (1.2cm) and fold in over the quilt edge (Fig 6). Fold the binding over to the back of the quilt and slip stitch in place (Fig 7). Make sure that the corners are really square before you stitch them.

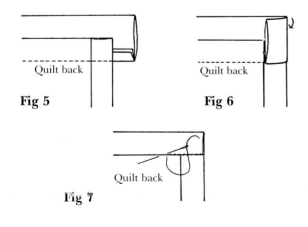

Quilt back

**Fig 5**

Quilt back

**Fig 6**

Quilt back

**Fig 7**

## LABELLING YOUR QUILT

Quilts should always have the maker's name and date of completion on it – you made it, so make sure future generations know its origins. On the back of the quilt or on a separate piece of fabric write your words either in pencil which will then be covered with stitches or with a Pigma pen, a fine felt pen that will not fade. Owners of hi-tech sewing machines can programme their machine to stitch a label for them while they make a cup of tea.

## QUILT CARE

The danger with making a rich and precious heirloom quilt is that you are afraid to use it and even more afraid to wash it. Don't worry too much: a well-made quilt will wash and wear wonderfully and if, in time, it shows signs of age that is part of its charm.

If your washing machine is large enough to hold the quilt comfortably, wash it with a low temperature programme and a mild washing agent. A short spin will remove some of the excess water and make the quilt less heavy.

If washing by hand, use the bath and agitate the quilt gently with your hands. Do not let it soak for any length of time. Rinse several times in the bath until the water runs clear. Press out as much water as you can while the quilt is still in the bath. Press towels against the quilt to absorb as much excess water as you can before removing it from the bath.

If possible dry the quilt flat, using a layer of towels or sheets underneath it. Another sheet on top will protect it from birds etc. Keep the quilt out of direct sunlight as this can fade the colours, even in Britain. Once dry, if it need to be pressed, use a cool iron without steam and just press the unquilted areas where creases may show. A hot iron can cause polyester batting to bond to the fabric, so use caution and test for the correct heat level for your particular quilt.

When the quilt is in use, beware of sunlight streaming through a bedroom window on to it. Even in temperate climes the sun fades fabric and can spoil a quilt, especially if only a section has been in the sun and it has faded in patches.

## A FINAL WORD. . .

Nobody *needs* to make a quilt: we do it because we love choosing fabric, handling fabric, arranging fabric and stitching fabric. It is not cheap. It is not quick. Sometimes it is not that well made. Most people cannot understand the pleasure it gives us. Remember – never give a quilt to someone who will not love it in the way you knows it deserves. Keep it yourself until the right owner comes along. That way everyone's happy and you can get busy on the next quilt. . .

## USEFUL ADDRESSES

### Associations and Publications

The Quilters' Guild
Room 190, Dean Clough
Halifax HX3 5AX
Tel: 01422 347669

International Quilting Times
Patchwork Association
Sackville Place
44–48 Magdalen Street
Norwich
Norfolk NR3 1JU
Tel: 01603 812259
E-mail: quiltex@webex.co.uk

*Patchwork and Quilting* Magazine
Traplet Publications Ltd
Traplet House, Severn Drive
Upton-Upon-Severn
Worcestershire WR8 0JL
Tel: 01684 594505
E-mail: general@traplet.co.uk

*Popular Patchwork* Magazine
Nexus Special Interests Ltd
Nexus House, Boundary Way
Hemel Hempstead
Hertfordshire HP2 7ST
Tel: 01322 660070

### Quilting Events and Activities

Details of current events are listed in the patchwork and quilting magazines. Addresses of contacts for local groups and clubs can usually be found in the local library, through the Quilters' Guild and from specialist quilt shops in your area.

### National Quilt Shows

Quilts UK and Quilts UK North
Grosvenor House Publishing Ltd
Grosvenor House, London Road
Spalding, Lincs PE11 2TN
Tel: 01775 712100/722900
E-mail: house@globalnet.co.uk

National Quilt Championships
Quilt Events
Sackville Place
44–48 Magdalen Street
Norwich
Norfolk NR3 1JU
Tel: 01603 629292
E-mail: quiltex@webex.co.uk

Knitting and Stitching Show
Creative Exhibitions Ltd
34 Lewisham Park
London SE13 6QZ
Tel: 0181 6908888
E-mail:
mail@eventorg.demon.co.uk

### Mail Order Patchwork and Quilting Supplies

The Cotton Patch
1285 Stratford Road, Hall Green
Birmingham B28 9AJ
Tel: 0800 0560509 or
0121 7022840
E-mail:
mailorder@cottonpatch.net

The Quilt Room
20 West Street
Dorking
Surrey RH4 1BL
Tel: 01306 877307

Strawberry Fayre
Chagford
Devon TQ13 8EN
Tel: 01647 433250

There are many quilt shops throughout the country that also do mail order. Refer to the patchwork and quilting magazines for details and advertisements of specialist shops.

## BIBLIOGRAPHY

CHAINEY, Barbara,
*The Essential Quilter*
(David and Charles, 1993)

DURCAN, Philomena,
*A Celtic Garden*
(Celtic Design Company, 1995)

EDIE, Marge,
*Bargello Quilts*
(That Patchwork Place, 1994)

EDWARDS, Lynne,
*The Sampler Quilt Book*
(David & Charles, 1996)

GREIDER BRADKIN, Cheryl,
*Basic Seminole Patchwork*
(C&T Publishing, 1990)

HARGRAVE, Harriet,
*Heirloom Machine Quilting*
(C&T Publishing, 1990)

HAYWOOD, Dixie & HALL, Jane,
*Firm Foundations*
(AQS Publications, 1996)

MARTIN, Judy & MCCLOSKEY, Marsha,
*Pieced Borders – The Complete Resource* (Crossley-Griffith, 1994)

MATHIESON, Judy,
*Mariner's Compass – New Directions*
(C&T Publications, 1995)

PAHL, Ellen,
*The Quilter's Ultimate Visual Guide*
(Rodale Books, 1997)

WALTON, Virginia A.,
*Creative Curves*
(Walton Publications, 1995)

## ACKNOWLEDGEMENTS

My thanks to the following people:

To Phyll Howes-Bassett, who insisted that a second, more advanced Sampler Quilt Course was needed.

To Barbara Chainey, who supplied advice and common sense when it was needed.

To Cheryl Brown, who waited patiently at David and Charles for me to be ready for this book, and to Lin Clements who made the editing painless and even enjoyable.

To the Staff at Hadleigh Library in Hadleigh, Suffolk for their interest and their willingness to hand over the key to the photocopier.

To all the quilters who allowed their quilts to be used in this book, and also to the quilters whose quilts were not included and who at least pretended to be magnanimous and understand that I just could not use everyone's quilt in the book.

# INDEX

Page numbers in *italics* indicate illustrations